So Many Miles for Mary

So Many Miles for Mary

The Story of an Epic Run

Philip David

MERTON PRIORY PRESS

First published 2003

Published by
Merton Priory Press Ltd
67 Merthyr Road, Whitchurch
Cardiff CF14 1DD

© Philip David 2003

Extracts from *Bruce Tulloh's Running Diary and Log, 1985*
(Tulloh & Tulloh, 1984) published by kind permission
of the author and publisher.

ISBN 1 898937 61 3

Printed by
Dinefwr Press
Rawlings Road, Llandybie
Carmarthenshire SA18 3YD

Contents

List of Illustrations

1

March 2002

Eighteen years ago, with the help of my wife, Megan, towing a caravan, I ran around mainland Britain to raise money for the Macmillan nurses.

The diaries and the story have lain untouched in our attic for over a decade. Now I have retired I have decided to organise myself and get it typed professionally and in book form. Reading through the story, I am quite astonished how we succeeded in only once losing touch with each other. It's difficult to imagine how we communicated so well with each other because no one had mobile phones in those days. Perhaps we were just lucky or skilled navigators!

So, when you read our story, remember everything was happening in 1984 not 2002.

1 Philip David's route round Britain.

8

2

Foreword

This is my story of an unusual journey around the mainland of Britain by my wife and me. It was undertaken more or less on the spur of the moment and with very little actual planning.

I hope it might interest other normal mortals, like myself, that ventures of this nature can be a success provided the individuals are prepared to take a few risks and not rely on outside support. So many things in life are often a gamble, and we must remember that opportunity knocks only once.

I would like to thank my family and friends for their enthusiasm and encouragement. This is what inspired me to succeed in the challenge I had set myself. Their faith in me gave me that extra will power and determination at the end of a long day when those few extra miles were needed.

I hope you will find our 2,354-mile, 70-day journey interesting. As you read it, remember that both my wife and I were a very ordinary middle-aged couple. I first took up running two and a half years ago and my wife is a newcomer to towing a caravan. She didn't once scratch either the car or the caravan and her navigation was excellent—with a couple of exceptions!

Finally, I would like to thank Bruce Tulloh for his advice and for lending me his book *Four Million Footsteps* which describes his epic, record breaking run across the USA in the summer of 1969. Apart from being a very interesting and well written book, it helped me to overcome a number of problems during my journey. Bruce holds the record for the long distance marathon run—Los Angeles to New York—of 2,876 miles. Time, 64 days, 21 hours, 50 minutes. He also won the gold medal in the 5,000 metres, European Athletic Championship of 1962. He ran bare footed!

Bruce very kindly includes a paragraph, in the introduction to his *Running Diary and Log of 1985*, referring to our story which I am about to relate.

Coincidentally, also during the summer of 1984, the famous cricketer Ian Botham (whose home town is also Yeovil) walked from John O'Groats to Land's End in aid of the Leukaemia charity. Like me, he too took 36 days but his route was more direct and shorter in distance—874 miles. My distance was 1,190 miles, but he was walking and I running!

3

Bruce Tulloh's Running Diary and Log, 1985

Introduction

The person who is going to be filling in this diary for the next twelve months is a little crazy. In the eyes of the world, anyone who tries to break out of the normal routine and make a bit of effort, with no financial gain, is crazy. We are, in our own way, idealists, looking for something better, trying to make ourselves into something better, and, like all idealists, we need heroes.

The most obvious heroes of 1984 were the Olympic winners. For the young runner, the heroes will be Daley Thompson, Seb Coe, Joachim Cruz or Shirley Strong. To win an Olympic title certainly demands great dedication as well as great talent. Daly Thompson holds all the major titles, not because he is a remarkable physical specimen but because he spares no effort in trying to improve. When he went to the Montreal Games at the age of seventeen he followed Bruce Jenner all around the village asking why he did this or that, never satisfied. It is the desire to do the thing well for its own sake, and to find the very best within yourself, that distinguishes the champion.

The older athletes amongst us would probably choose as our Olympic heroes either Joyce Smith or Carlos Lopes, for their mental toughness in continuing to pursue their Olympic ideal at an age when most people have settled for the easy life. The fact that Lopes, only a couple of years away from being a veteran, can break the world ten thousand metres record, win the world cross country championships and the toughest Olympic marathon, opens up new vistas for the thirty year old runner who is thinking it's about time to ease off.

One of my heroes died last year. Although I met Jim Fixx only a couple of times, I saw enough of him to know that here was a man who believed in doing things properly and getting the very best out of himself in every sphere. He became rich and famous not by design, but because the book he wrote was one which was needed, and was very well written. His running career was not successful in the conventional sense, but it was successful in one very important way, in that he lived ten years longer than his father. It may have been this feeling that life is short that gave him the philosophical attitude to life. He was able to laugh at himself, and at the things that happened to him. He had the ability to take seriously the things he did, without taking himself too seriously.

My real hero of 1984, however, is not famous or rich. Through *Running* magazine I come into contact with all sorts of runners, of all ages and abilities. Philip David from Yeovil differs from the average runner only in being somewhat older—he took it up when past fifty and built up to running a three and a half hour marathon. At this point most people would feel satisfied and settle down to maintaining fitness, but Philip went on ... and on. Last summer he completed a 2,354-mile trip round Britain at an average of over thirty miles a day. The speed may not have been great but that meant doing more than a marathon every day for 10 weeks, a feat which you might think about when you are filling in your weekly mileage.

The 1985 Diary is the second of what I hope will be an annual event. The monthly Calendar of Events owes a good deal to *Running* magazine, which continues to be the flag bearer of the boom (if booms have flags!), but it is not their fault that it is not comprehensive. Since we went to press in August 1984, it has not been easy to get organisers to commit themselves to dates for their 1985 events. A Diary, obviously, is as valuable as the diarist makes it, but I hope that there is sufficient stimulation in my articles to get you thinking about your running—where it is going and why—and if you feel like writing to tell me about it I shall be delighted to get some feedback.

Have a good 1985.

Bruce Tulloh

4

The Beginning of the End

It was just after 6 a.m. on Friday 27 July 1984 that I set off in the early morning mist to run the final leg of a 2,354-mile marathon. The evening before we had been fortunate in finding a picnic area situated well off the dual carriageway. We were now in Dorset and a couple of miles south of Ringwood and on the edge of Ringwood Forest. I was particularly grateful for this peaceful location for our final night's camping site as I didn't expect sleep would come easily. There was an air of excitement in the knowledge that we were now only 22 miles from our final goal. As I tried to sleep my mind recalled various incidents during our 69-day journey. Crossing Dartmoor on my 56th birthday and celebrating it with a trout supper. Leaping into the hedge near Minehead, to avoid a lorry, nearly giving up at the approaches to the Severn Bridge and jumping on an adder near John O'Groats!

I was feeling thankful that the task was near its end. I was beginning to tire mentally and, although I didn't feel physically exhausted, I knew my body was beginning to rebel at the constant punishment. My hips had been quite stiff for the last three or four days and I often wished it was possible to give them an injection of '3-in-1' oil. In the heat of the day, like a mirage or a dream, I enjoyed imagining I could see in the sky ahead of me, a hot bath floating by, followed by a feather bed. You don't get either of these luxuries in a caravan. Well, not ours anyway!

At 8.30 a.m. I caught up with Megan in a convenient lay-by and we had our usual breakfast of grapefruit, cereal, toast and a glass of milk. By now it was beginning to get quite warm and we were pleased to think that the venture would end in sunshine. We had informed Commander Nash that we would arrive at Wool Post Office at noon, and we set about planning to get there at exactly the correct time. We assumed the Navy would be dead on time! At breakfast we decided to keep going, without a break, until we reached a convenient lay by in Wareham. There I could rest before making the final four- or five-mile run to the finishing line. As it turned out, there were very few lay bys on this stretch of road, and at one stage I thought I was taking the wrong road. There were a lot of road alterations on the outskirts of Bournemouth and Poole. For some reason it seemed a very long and lonely stretch to run. It was also becoming very hot and I wished I could throw away my singlet as the sweat was running off me in rivers. It was difficult to believe that we had almost completed the circuit and would soon be arriving back in Wool, where we had left 70 days ago on 18 May.

I was very thankful to find the caravan parked near the centre of Wareham, and I very quickly sank several glasses of lemonade and orange juice. With just five miles to go I had time for a good 20 minutes rest. It's strange, but it's difficult to remember much about that last lap. I know I was thinking about my parents and how pleased and surprised they would be if they had been able to witness no. 5 son jogging back to base after a 70-day run. I was also thinking of those relatives and friends who had supported me throughout. Suddenly I was approaching the outskirts of Wool. It was 11.45 a.m. and I could see Megan and the caravan ahead in a queue of cars. The road was closed for the London train and it looked as though it might interfere with our carefully calculated arrival time. Fortunately, the gates soon lifted and, with the sun still beating down, I followed Megan and the caravan through Wool towards the finishing line at the Post Office Stores. At exactly noon I turned the final corner and I could see a small reception committee awaiting my arrival. My main concern at this point was that someone would hopefully produce a pint of lemonade or shandy to quench my thirst!

5

The Challenge

24 May 1982 was quite an ordinary day apart from the fact that it happened to be my 54th birthday. When I was a small boy I was often told by my favourite aunt how fortunate I was to share my birthday with Queen Victoria. Actually I was far more delighted that it was also my aunt's birthday. In my youth 24 May was celebrated as 'Empire Day' and we had a half day's holiday from school which my friend and I usually spent bird nesting. (In those days egg collecting was a popular and acceptable boys' hobby; quite rightly, the activity has since been banned.) My 1982 birthday was a very quiet affair and enabled me to add to my growing stockpile of handkerchiefs, socks and ties (I doubt if this passage will ever get printed). Fortunately, both my daughters were home for the day and helped Megan cook a grand evening meal which we washed down with a bottle of wine. It was during the good humoured remarks that flow on these occasions that Nicola, our second daughter, happened to quip—'at your age Dad, you'll be over the hill now'.

This remark must have lodged somewhere in my subconscious and on Sunday 30 May I sneaked off in the car with a pair of shorts and an old pair of tennis shoes—pumps we used to call them. I was determined to have a go at running. I hadn't liked the 'over the hill' remark—probably because it was fairly near the truth! At 4 p.m. I was all set to smash through the 10-minute mile barrier. Sadly there were no witnesses to this knee knocking sprint through the country-side. I had measured the course with the car mileometer and the timing device was my wristwatch with its broken second hand. The mile seemed a very long way and I struggled over the finishing line in something just over 12 minutes. I was sweating, breathless and exhausted. When I look back at it now I realise I was foolish to run so far at the first attempt. I should have jogged gently for no more than five minutes. The following morning I was actually stiff.

I spent the next few days in a very depressed state of mind. I couldn't understand what it was that I was trying to prove, and in any event a 12-minute mile was a disgrace! It set me thinking about running. What should a man of my age be capable of attaining? Until now I hadn't been interested in running and certainly hadn't bothered to watch the London Marathon on TV, but I remembered how much I had enjoyed a month at the Outward Bound Sea School in Aberdovey in the spring of 1945. I quickly searched through my accumulated years of hoarding personal papers and discovered my athletics report of that particular course. The 100 yards I completed in 14.8 seconds, which I recall with embarrassment, was about the slowest on record for my age group, and probably still is! However, I found some encouragement in the two-mile event which I ran in 12 minutes 39 seconds, and for this I gained a silver award. This information transformed my depression to optimism and I decided that there must be some latent talent somewhere in my skinny physique. I hoped it would be just a matter of persevering until it would finally surface.

Early in June I was back jogging along the roads with my tennis shoes. I really had no idea what I was doing, but began to measure my improvement by seeing how many telegraph poles I could pass before having to stop for a rest. It took me about a week before I could pass ten! Towards the end of June I obtained my first *Running* magazine and I was very fortunate to find it included a 52-week training schedule for beginners wishing to attempt a marathon. I didn't know anything about marathon running but it seemed to be some sort of target to aim for, so I ordered Cliff Temple's *Challenge of the Marathon* from my local library. By the first week of July I had already decided that I wanted to run a marathon, and from what I had read, the greatest fun run event must be the London Marathon.

Now that I had a definite goal I began to make plans and suddenly there seemed to be a purpose in what I was doing. At this point I was able to run for 15 minutes without stopping.

I had now set my heart on running in the London Marathon on 17 April 1983, and decided to plan accordingly. Looking at the beginners' 52-week schedule I realised I would have to rewrite it because I was at least six weeks behind in performance. I set off one evening in the car with a pot of white paint and a brush and marked out a number of routes from my home that I intended using over the next nine months. Hopefully the local people living near Wincanton will now understand the figures they may have seen painted on the sides of the roads! Appreciating that it would be quite a tough training programme, and that it was very important to be 100 per cent fit before attempting this marathon, I decided to make, and keep, three basic rules:

1 Unless I felt unwell I would run each day regardless of weather conditions.

2 I would not stop during a training run, however long it was. The only exception being if I felt unwell. Tiredness was not an exception!

3 I would regularly monitor my times over the various routes. This was only to gauge my natural improvement due to training. I would never attempt to run faster (this might come at a very much later stage in training).

As this was now becoming a serious matter I decided to treat myself to buying some real running shoes. Then, with a pair of 'Silver Shadows' on my feet I conceitedly considered I was slowly progressing from a jogger to a runner. After all, by the end of July, I could run five miles without stopping in just over 40 minutes. At this stage I didn't allow my mind to even think beyond ten miles, but I had entered my first public event of twelve and a half miles at Somerton on 19 September.

During the month of August I quickly progressed from my longest Sunday run of five miles to one of nearly eleven miles. It had seemed easier to make this improvement than it had been to move up from the half mile to the five mile distance which had been quite a strain. I was now reaching a point where even my short runs were in excess of half an hour and it was necessary to adjust my working timetable to fit in with these daily runs. Fortunately, I rarely went home for lunch so I could usually fit something in during the 1–2 p.m. period. My actual lunch usually consisted of a pint of milk, an apple and a small piece of cheese. I was now looking forward to entering this first event on 19 September. As the date approached I relaxed my training for the last couple of days and felt quite fit but rather nervous when I actually lined up in the town square of Somerton. The weather was fine and I thoroughly enjoyed myself and managed to talk to quite a few other competitors. I was also very pleased to find that I had completed the course of twelve and a half miles in 1.37.27, which was the first time I had achieved under eight minute miling. And there were quite a few finishers coming in behind me.

I think there were two main lessons I learned from this race:

1 Without necessarily attempting to do so, one will run slightly faster in a group of people than on an equivalent training distance, when running by oneself.

2 Not to attempt racing these distances unless the appropriate training has been undertaken.

In exactly four weeks I was due to run in my first half marathon at Longleat. Unfortunately, after the Somerton run, I had a slight injury and did very little training for the next couple of weeks. That left a fortnight to prepare for my second race. The grounds of Longleat were in a very pleasant setting for the start and finish of this half marathon. I felt quite fit and relaxed as we set off on our first circuit but found the first mile quite an uphill struggle. By the half way stage I was already tired and dreading the hilly circuit for the second time. At about eleven miles I was quite prepared to offer myself as an early lunch to one of the Longleat lions, but unfortunately none of them were in sight. I completed this course in 1.52.15, which was well over eight-minute miling, and I was very, very tired. I was wrong. I hadn't really learned the lesson of training properly for this run. After that fortnight's injury I wasn't quite ready for this event. Sometimes there is no alternative but to learn from experience. I'll always remember the two young ladies who came in about a minute ahead of me. I had been running just behind them for most of the race and they had continued chatting away, ten to the dozen, even up the steep hills. They seemed oblivious of other competitors or their surroundings and their language was something I couldn't forget!

The following week I only ran a few miles and it gave me the opportunity to consider carefully what I had learned from my first two races and how I should plan and adjust my training in order to reach a peak for the London Marathon on 17 April. I believed I had now almost caught up with the 52-week training programme which I had obtained from *Running* magazine. Up to the present I felt this training had served me quite well and it seemed to suit my style of running on my own. I had no wish to join any particular running groups, although I'm sure there would have been many advantages. In some ways I'm a bit of a 'loner'. Due to illness I lost two more valuable weeks of training in early November but was cheered by the fact that I felt fairly confident that I had been well placed in the Post Office queue to guarantee an early date stamp on my London Marathon entry form. A group of us had been queuing in turn for 24 hours and it had been quite a cold night. By Christmas I had settled down again to my daily running routine and a place for me in the London Marathon had been confirmed. It was the spur I needed. I was now very determined not to fail in this challenge that I had set myself. Although very inexperienced, I felt confident that I could succeed if I stuck rigidly to the training schedule that I had been following for the last five months. I was now reaching a point where I was regularly running distances of over ten miles, and sometimes 15 miles. However, the idea of completing a non-stop course of 26 miles and 385 yards was frightening!

Fortunately the winter months were not too harsh and only rarely did the weather threaten to interfere with my training schedule. I often used to think I was very lucky because it seldom seemed to rain on a Sunday morning when I usually set off for my long run, but no sooner had I got home than the rains came down. On once occasion it began to snow when I rounded my furthest point from home — about six miles out in a country lane — and I'd forgotten my gloves! I had two races planned before April. The first one was the 'Alweston 10' on 6 March and the second one was the 'Bath Half Marathon' on 20 March. These two runs seemed ideally suited as 'build ups' for the main event in April, and the time intervals just about perfect.

I was really looking forward to the 'Alweston 10' to see how much I had improved during the winter months. I had now run several 15-mile training sessions and one of 17 miles, and all of them just under eight minute miling. 6 March was one of those cold, crisp, sunny mornings and I could see and feel the goose pimples on my knobbly knees. I felt blue with the cold and didn't enjoy the long wait before we eventually lined up for the start. I very quickly forgot the cold and soon settled down to my normal training pace, and after about a mile people stopped passing me — not that there were many left behind me anyway. I don't remember very much about this particular run, except that I was very surprised at my finishing time of 73.17. The two young ladies from Longleat were running, and still talking! But this time I came in ahead of them. This was well under seven and a half minute miling. I hadn't tried to run any faster than normal training sessions but obviously one tends gradually to catch the next competitor ahead, and then the next one afterwards and so on. And so, presumably, you get pulled along at a slightly faster pace than you expect. So far so good, and my first marathon was now only six weeks away, with one more competitive half marathon at Bath in a fortnight.

I discovered that Martin, Megan's cousin's 18-year-old son, was running in this event and so it was arranged that I would travel to their home to change and we would both go off to the start point together. Naturally there was a lot of friendly rivalry as to who would emerge winner between the two of us. Martin was physically very well developed and looked as though he possessed plenty of natural stamina. On the other hand, he didn't seem to have done very much training—or the amount he had done would have got me no further than a couple of miles. Unfortunately we got separated at the start and I thought I wouldn't see him again. However, at about the one mile mark he appeared at my side and politely offered me a glucose energy tablet, with a grin on his face. I think he thought I needed it!

It was almost depressing to see him glide ahead with such youthful ease. Nevertheless, I began to settle down and feel that I was running quite well, and the miles passed by quite quickly. Only the drizzle was spoiling it as a spectator event. I think it was just after the 11-mile marker that I caught sight of Martin, who was then about 50 yards ahead of me. That really cheered me up and I set about closing that gap being determined that it would be me who would cross the line first. It's surprising how long it takes to close a gap of 50 yards. It must have been another mile before I drew alongside him and unkindly asked if he'd saved anything for the final sprint! My finishing time was 96.38, with which I was well pleased, and it hadn't left me too exhausted. Martin came in about two minutes after me. Looking back, with a little more experience, I think it quite astonishing that an 18-year-old could complete a half marathon in under 100 minutes on virtually no training other than school sports. I admired him for his stubborn courage during the last few miles as I'm sure it must have been difficult to place one foot in front of the other. Anyway, we returned to Martin's house and enjoyed a wonderful Sunday lunch and I'm sure both Martin and I were delighted to have shared in such an exciting fun run together.

Just four more weeks before I was to be put to the test—or to the sword! I was now taking particular care not to deviate from the running schedule. It had served me well so far and it would be foolish to introduce any fresh ideas. I had no experience of my own to fall back on. Sometimes it had been difficult to fit in the longer midweek runs and there were occasions when I had been working late in the evening and had returned to our Yeovil office as late as 11 p.m., changed into running gear and spent the next one and a half hours running around the lighted streets. Saturday 2 April I ran my first 20 miles in a training session, and this was to be my longest run before attempting the actual marathon distance of 26 miles. I ran this 20 miles in 2.36.40 which again was just under eight minutes per mile. But I was quite tired and couldn't help wondering how difficult it was going to be to add another six miles on top of the 20. I decided not to think about it and therefore shut it out of my mind.

From this point onwards, with 14 days to go, the training sessions became shorter. It was more important to rest and build up strength for the big day. I've never had a large appetite but, as the last week approached, I tried to increase the protein intake and then, during the final four days, I switched to carbohydrate. I've no idea whether it helped me physically, but I'm sure it did mentally.

With only three days to go I caught a cold. I had a sore throat and felt hot and flushed. This was quite a problem because I'd read how important it was *not* to run if not feeling 100 per cent fit. I had so set my mind on running in the London Marathon and I didn't believe I could ever sustain the necessary weeks of training all over again. I decided to carry on and, if necessary, call it off at the last moment. I started to stuff myself with honey and hot lemon and Vitamin C tablets, also hot baths, which was probably quite foolish.

On Saturday we drove up to London. My niece had just recently left London to live temporarily in Norway and had very kindly offered us her flat in Dolphin Square. This meant that Megan and our two daughters, Nicola and Sarah, were able to come as well. We arrived in London at about 11 a.m., which gave me plenty of time to register at the County Hall before lunch.

After lunch I went for a two-mile gentle jog and fed myself some more honey and lemon and vitamin C tablets. Just after 6 p.m. we ordered a taxi to take us to the Royal Lancaster Hotel where 'Record' Pasta Foods had organised a massive pasta party. We had to queue in the street for about ten minutes before we could get near the refresh-ments. The hotel was packed with hundreds of competitors and friends, taking aboard their last helpings of carbohydrate loading, Guinness and pasta foods. We didn't stay long but, like everybody else, felt the pre-race excitement and enjoyed ourselves immensely. Then, after yet another hot bath, I decided to relax and see how I felt in the morning.

The alarm woke me at 5.30 a.m. on Sunday 17 April. It was the day I had been waiting for, and training for, since June of last year. I decided I didn't feel too much under the weather, maybe not 100 per cent fit, but fairly close to it, and if I didn't feel well during the run I could always drop out. I decided I would run and, having made that decision, I confirmed the taxi appointment and settled down to my last breakfast—fruit juice, cornflakes, toast and honey. A taxi arrived a little after 7 a.m. and took me to Charing Cross. As soon as I disembarked I realised that the station was packed with thousands of runners of all nationalities. Probably many of them, like me, were nervous and apprehensive, and about to attempt their first marathon. It was a lonely feeling, and yet among so many people.

The 20-minute journey down to Greenwich seemed endless and the carriage was full of younger competitors who were obviously accomplished runners. Greenwich station was a dismal sight as there seemed to be thousands of runners milling about in the pouring rain. I quickly found a seat in a corner of one of the waiting rooms and watched spellbound as these competitors began to prepare for this great event. Within minutes the place began to smell like a chemist's shop. I was fascinated to see how many different ointments were used and wondered what I had been missing. Suddenly I was approached by a tall, athletic Scotsman who looked like a wing forward with his sweatband and formidable figure. He was offering me some lotion to rub into my calf muscles. I couldn't very well refuse and decided it was time, anyway, to strip off my track suit and look for those muscles of mine. However, I was already sufficiently experienced to realise that I had very many advantages with a small frame and only eight and a half stone to transport over this vast distance.

It would soon be time to make tracks for the start line, so I dashed off to join the queue for a last visit to the loo. It wasn't a very comfortable sight to see about 20 people ahead for each loo. If you think about it, Greenwich Station wasn't built to accommodate thousands of nervous runners all anxious for a last visit. When my turn finally arrived I discovered my journey wasn't really necessary and all it did was to set me off to the start line in a panic as everyone else seemed to have suddenly disappeared. I arrived with about five minutes to spare and threw my bag containing tracksuit etc. into the 'C' bus instead of the 'D' bus. It was still drizzling and I felt ridiculous in my black rubbish bag that we had all put over our heads. I was feeling quite hot and flushed and decided I would take drinks at each and every opportunity.

Once I had lined up with the other 8,000 competitors I began to relax and enjoy the atmosphere. I no longer felt nervous or apprehensive — it was too late anyhow. I knew I had trained exactly as the experts had advised and therefore I should be confident in at least completing the course and, being realistic, my training results projected a finishing time of between three and a half and four hours.

The one advantage of being a late arrival was that I only had about three minutes to wait until 9.30, before the Royal Artillery sixteen pounder field gun at Greenwich boomed to start the 1983 London Marathon. My immediate thoughts were … I wonder where I'll be at 2 p.m. today.

Just before the start I had struck up a conversation with a young lady from Cumbria. Although she was only 20, it was not her first marathon and it was helpful to have the company of an experienced runner for at least the start of the adventure. Carolyn Etheridge came from Carlisle and for her it was a family event because her father was also running. As we set off in the drizzle we discarded our black rubbish bags but it was about three and a half minutes after the gun fired before we actually crossed over the starting line, and then only at a very gentle jog. It was bound to be a bit crowded with 8,000 runners and I wondered what it would be like when the other 8,000 who had started in Shooters Hill Road, converged after about two and a half miles.

Already everyone seemed to be totally relaxed and thoroughly enjoying themselves. The runners were joking with one another and the crowds lining the streets were singing and shouting encouragement. For a period the helicopters were buzzing about overhead, presumably photographing this army of hopeful marathon runners. It must have been a wonderful sight to look down from above at 16,000 men and women of all sorts and sizes and with such colourful running attire.

The first three or four miles were quite slow, but from that point onwards it was possible to set our own pace. At times the roads were very crowded with runners and it was necessary to take care not to trip or, alternatively, to trip another competitor. Carolyn and I seemed to have much the same pace and we decided to run together for as long as it suited us. We took it in turn to snatch the plastic cups with our electrolyte drinks whilst the other ran in the centre of the road.

The atmosphere of the crowd, and the competitors, is difficult to describe—everyone just seemed so happy and thoroughly enjoying the Sunday outing. My head was feeling hotter than it should have done so I was delighted with the light drizzle which I'm sure helped me a great deal. Keeping our eyes on the road and the other competitors it was difficult to recognise the surroundings. It became easier as the race progressed. The streets became wider and the runners began to thin out a little. I enjoyed running alongside the *Cutty Sark* and seeing Sir Francis Chichester's *Gypsy Moth IV*. The *Cutty Sark* was an old friend as I had scrubbed her decks on many occasions 40 years before when I had been a cadet on the pre-sea training ship HMS *Worcester*. The school itself was called the Thames National Training College and was based at Ingress Abbey at Greenhithe. The *Cutty Sark* and the old wooden battleship HMS *Worcester* were moored in the river off Greenhithe. An extract from *The Colonial Clippers* shows the importance of loading as many bales of wool as was possible during the height of the Australian wool trade:

> As showing how much the amount of wool loaded depended upon the captain. Captain Woodgate used to get 1,000 bales more into the *Cutty Sark* than his predecessor. He made a habit of spending most of the day in the ship's hold and thought nothing of having a tier or half longer pulled down and restowed if he was not satisfied with the number of bales got in.

> You can dunnage casks o' tallow; you can handle hides an' horn;
> You can carry frozen mutton; you can lumber sacks o' corn;
> But the queerest kind o' cargo that you've got to haul and pull
> Is Australia's 'staple product'—is her God abandoned wool.
> For it's greasy an' it's stinkin', an' them awkward ugly bales
> Must be jammed as close as herrings in a ship afore she sails.
> For it's twist the screw and turn it,
> And the bit you get you earn it.
> You can take the tip from me, sir, that it's anything but play
> When you're layin' on the screw,

When you're draggin' on the screw,
In the summer, under hatches, in the middle o' the day.

It seemed no time at all before we were crossing over Tower Bridge and heading eastwards towards the Isle of Dogs. The crowds seemed endless and on both sides of the road. We reached the half way point of 13.1 miles soon after crossing Tower Bridge in 1.52.00 which was slower than I had expected, but otherwise everything was fine. It was really wonderful to see so many happy people and already I was believing that it wasn't possible to fail with such an encouraging crowd.

The difficult points came somewhere between 17 and 22 miles. By 17 miles Carolyn and I had decided that, as we had survived together for this distance, we would try to stick together for the remainder of the course. I think this was a sensible, and not just a friendly decision as it gave confidence to both of us that the other was concerned that it should be a successful venture for both of us. Both of us in turn went through a slightly difficult period somewhere around the 20-mile mark. The encouragement of a friend at this point can be very valuable and I know it did help me. By 22 miles we were both very tired but I think we now knew we had been through the worst of it and could sustain and maintain our pace for the next four miles. We stopped talking and concentrated carefully on completing this mission.

It was quite an emotional feeling as those final miles melted away. I found it difficult to believe that I was running through Trafalgar Square and The Mall, with thousands of people cheering. It might seem conceited but I felt they were cheering for me and, as I've never achieved a feat anything remotely like running a marathon, you can imagine the warm feeling I felt inside. Next we were passing Queen Victoria's Memorial and Buckingham Palace and turning into Birdcage Walk. There was less than a mile to go. With the crowd singing 'only five minutes more', the emotional relief, with success almost in sight, was difficult to contain. Those months of training had really been worthwhile.

As we approached the Houses of Parliament and Westminster Bridge I turned to look up at Big Ben and the time seemed frozen at five minutes past one, and a little misty. I knew we would cross the finishing line together in under 3.40.00. I hardly remember the actual finish but I remember the feeling of relief and the joy of being able to share the success with someone else. It wasn't the personal success that was important but the memory of a truly happy occasion where thousands of other people gave immense pleasure to one another. There can not be many sports where people of all shapes, sizes and age groups can compete on equal terms. Carolyn and I were of the opposite sex and 34 years apart in age. We completed our marathon in 3.38.53 and we should feel proud of the fact that we were just 20 seconds behind the Gurkhas! And we ran the second half three minutes faster than the first half. Carolyn and I have not met since that day in 1983 but she has written every Christmas since, sending photographs of her growing family.

Megan and our two daughters had managed to spot me somewhere near the 20-mile mark. I didn't see them, which wasn't surprising, but at least from their point of view they knew I hadn't dropped out. They too had enjoyed the outing and were looking forward to some sort of celebration later in the day. It took quite a long time to get back to the flat and, after yet another hot bath, I was ready for a stiff drink. My cold hadn't been any sort of handicap, but on balance I might have taken an unwise risk.

Soon after our return from the London exploit I was looking ahead to another marathon. Having now satisfied myself that I could actually complete a marathon, I was interested in how much faster I could run. To please my elder sister I picked the Dartmoor Marathon, due to be run on Sunday 11 September. I liked the idea myself because I knew the local countryside and there would be friends and relatives to give me the necessary encouragement. In many ways it wasn't a very bright idea if my main aim was to improve my marathon time. The Dartmoor course had three very steep hills and it seemed likely to me that it might take nearer four hours to complete. Anyway, the die was cast, and I had also agreed to run for a local charity, the Dartmoor Livestock Protection Society. My sister was a committee member of this society. This produced local interest in Tavistock and eventually I reached the front page of the *Tavistock Gazette*. Now I had to succeed. In the London Marathon I had raised about £400 for two separate charities—the RNLI and Cancer Research. I wondered how much I would raise for the DLPS.

My training pattern was much the same as for the London Marathon but I did try running faster in training and attempted special hilly routes at least once a week. In August I entered the British Veteran Championships at Melksham and ran in the 10,000 metres event. I was quite pleased with my time of 42.44.5, which was under seven

2 The author completing the Dartmoor Marathon, September 1983.

minute miling. On Saturday 27 August I ran a 20-mile training run in two and a half hours and this was my long run prior to the Dartmoor Marathon.

We started the course near Sir Francis Drake's statue in Tavistock, climbing steadily out of the town on to the golf course, and eventually joined the A384 south of Cox Tor. The route continued uphill past

Merrivale quarry and on to Rendlestone where we turned off towards Princetown. The huge, grey stone Dartmoor prison was a depressing sight and I wondered whether the unfortunate inmates were watching our ordeal. We turned south on the B3212 towards Yelverton but took a detour around Burrator Reservoir where the scenery was beautiful. After Horrabridge we had one more steep hill before finally completing the circuit by freewheeling through Whitchurch and back to the finishing line in Tavistock.

I was delighted to complete it in 3.28.59 and felt very superior to be a couple of places ahead of Sally Cronshaw, the first lady home, particularly as she'd beaten me in the London Marathon. I was placed 74 out of a finishing field of 208 runners.

My next target was to gain a special certificate in my age group from the Road Runners Club. To achieve this I would have to:

    a run a marathon in under 3.25
    b the 'Salisbury Plain 15 ½ miles' in 1.55.00 and
    c the 'AP20' in 2.30.00.

As a build-up to these three events I entered the Sherborne half marathon and was delighted to complete it in 1.31.55, failing by only five yards to gain a prize for the first man in the over-50 age group. However, I wasn't so fortunate in the Salisbury Plain 15½ as I arrived at the finishing line just seven seconds too late. After running for nearly two hours there is an understandable feeling of disappointment to fail by so small a margin. I must have fallen asleep in the AP20 as I was over a minute outside the required time. Perhaps, at last, I was over the hill!

After the London Marathon I wrote to the RNLI and suggested the idea of running a relay right around the UK coast—pairs of runners covering a distance of about 15–20 miles and then handing a baton on to the next pair. The main lifeboat stations, or a selected number of them, would be visited by these relay runners en route. I envisaged it would take about 50 days to complete the UK circuit provided they could run from dawn to dusk with the appropriate back-up vehicles. The reply I eventually received from the RNLI was not very encouraging. They thought it both too difficult and too expensive to organise.

As the winter approached I began to have a ridiculous idea. On Tuesday 6 December I took a day off work and at 6 a.m. set off and ran five miles. At 9.30 a.m. I did seven miles and at 2.45 p.m. seven miles, 5 p.m. two miles and at 8.30 p.m. another seven miles. A total for the day of 28 miles. Yes, the idea I had in mind could be a possibility provided I could find the time.

The secret of making something work in your life is the deep desire to make it work. You need the faith and belief that it can work, and also a vision in your mind to see it working out step by step without any doubt that it will fail. There's an interesting, or perhaps appropriate, Buddhist saying: 'If we are facing in the correct direction, all we have to do is to keep on walking'. In my case I will need to substitute 'running' for 'walking'!

6

En Route to Lizard Point and Land's End

During January and February I eased up a little on my running, but still managed to average a steady 25–30 miles per week. I was quite satisfied to feel that I was at least ticking over. It was a busy period for me with my work and we were also endeavouring to sell our property in Wincanton and move into Yeovil. I had by now decided that I would like to attempt running around the coastline of Britain with Megan supporting me with some sort of back-up vehicle. I appreciated that we would have to pay for the venture ourselves as there was no likelihood of receiving any outside financial assistance. Whether or not this idea got off the ground was obviously dependant on two main factors, namely opportunity and a very mean budget.

When I first started to seek advice my optimism and enthusiasm began to wane. I was told I would need several months of special long daily training sessions to harden my feet and to gain the extra stamina that I would require if I intended to run over 30 miles daily and continually for nearly three months. Furthermore, I would need to study and plan the routes and roads over which I would have to run. There were numerous questions which required answers. Where were we going to park at nights? How would we manage to keep up with the washing of my running clothes as I would need to change many times each day? Had I thought of the need for regular hot baths? Had I considered the dangers of running on main roads? Our roads are not built for joggers or runners and, over such a long distance, passing through large cities and various industrial belts, there must be occasions when a runner would be at risk. How does the runner and the back-up vehicle keep in touch when journeying through these industrial belts and complex road networks? What happens if and when we lose touch with each other? Mobile phones were not an option in 1984!

I was beginning to feel that things were getting out of hand and although the advice I had received sounded both sensible and necessary I knew that if I tried to follow it I would never leave the starting grid. We would just have to revert to accepting the opportunity when it arose and tackle it with a budget that wouldn't alarm our bank manager! I was beginning to shut out of my mind some of the obvious problems and worries. I sensed we would succeed but I didn't know how. Perhaps I was suffering from tunnel vision, which Megan frequently asserts is among my many problems! In any event I just didn't have the experience or knowledge of my own running capabilities to extensively plan anything. I didn't feel competent or confident that I could succeed in running for more than a few days. However, I was very determined to have a go and I'd just have to train as we went along.

Although I was very nervous and apprehensive about the whole project I hoped my stubborn streak and resolve to succeed would overcome any difficulties. I didn't possess any sensible plans or arguments to satisfy the experts so I decided to crawl back into my shell and work out the problems and plans as best I could. It is sometimes very difficult to explain one's inner feelings. Although I sensed that I could succeed in the challenge I had set myself it wasn't conceit as I didn't believe I was a good runner or possessed a particularly suitable physique. But I did believe it was a mental attitude. The situation provided me with an opportunity to achieve something that a few years earlier I would have considered impossible. Secondly, I had the inspiration, which was a very important driving force, and finally, I have a cowardly streak of being afraid of failing.

So, with this tunnel vision and inspiration the die was cast. The month of May had arrived and I felt it was imperative that we should set off early in the second half of the month. Fortunately we had just exchanged contracts for the sale of our house and we had viewed a suitable property in Yeovil. At this point we started looking at various second hand caravanettes. The important essentials were cooking facilities and a lavatory as we intended camping by the roadside and not relying on camping sites. Besides, it was important to keep our expenses down to a minimum. It soon became apparent that a reasonable second hand caravanette was going to cost between £3,000 and £4,000 and I considered this too risky an investment. I visualised losing at least £1,000 when we came to sell it at the end of the sum-

3 Our home! Car, caravan (with Macmillan Cancer Relief adverts on the side) and Merlin.

mer. We then turned our attention to caravans and I think we were very lucky in finding a Knowsley two berth with heater, cooker, lavatory and refrigerator. We struck a good deal with the purchase price of £625. We did spend a further £50 on a few general repairs, electrical faults and servicing. Megan was very nervous at the prospect of towing a caravan through the busy and narrow roads of Devon and Cornwall and, understandably, she would have preferred a caravanette. Unkindly, I let her worry about Devon and Cornwall—I was more concerned about the roads in the Highlands of Scotland! I might have the physical struggle to cope with but Megan was taking on a considerable responsibility, and a worrying one at that, in attempting to tow a caravan not only through the narrow roads of Devon and Cornwall but the remote Highlands of Scotland and complicated industrial belts such as South Wales, the Midlands and Tyneside. I was very fortunate in having such a game partner for this venture. Furthermore, towing a caravan was a new experience for Megan. There were going to be more that one or two worrying incidents. At this point I wrote again to the RNLI and asked them if they were interested in raising money on my proposed Round the Coast of Britain Run. They were not interested so I got in touch with Commander Nash who was the regional manager of the Macmillan Cancer

Relief Fund. He was disappointed that I intended setting off so soon as it didn't really give him sufficient time to organise his 'helpers' in the south west region. However, he sent me half a dozen running vests with 'Macmillan Cancer Relief Fund' written on the front and on the back and agreed to see me off on Friday 10 May at noon from Wool Post Office in Dorset. I decided that we should aim to reach the most northerly, southerly, easterly and westerly points of the kingdom and the routes in between should be those that were most suitable for the caravan. These four cardinal points were Dunnet Head, about 15 miles west of John O'Groats, Lizard Point, Lowestoft and Land's End. Actually there are several points in Scotland that are not easily accessible by caravan a little further west than Land's End. Where we turned north off the A87 just east of the Kyle of Lochalsh was a point possibly just a little further to the west than Land's End, but our first target would be Lizard Point.

We had set a date and the caravan had been overhauled and repaired where necessary. I now had to convince Megan just how simple it would be to find lay-bys every three or four miles! So, on Sunday 13 May, with just five days to D-Day, we set off for Wool with the car only to plan our first three night stops en route for Lizard Point, taking care to note the lay-bys for pull ins during the day rest periods.

When we arrived in Wool we reset our mileometer and set off in the direction of Exeter, making the necessary notes as the miles ticked by. After a lot of discussion we eventually picked our sites for the first three nights and hoped everything would go according to plan. The lay-bys were not as convenient as I had hoped but there would be many occasions when I would have to run further than anticipated. Megan was more apprehensive at the end of our trip than she had been at the beginning and, secretly, I would not have described my own feelings as being very confident.

The next four days were spent stocking the caravan with food etc., writing various letters and packing all our household furniture into one room. There was no time to do any running but I suppose dragging beds, chests of drawers and trunks from bedrooms and the attic rooms to the ground floor was some sort of training.

On the Thursday I had to dash off to Swindon for a sales meeting. One of those affairs where the better salesmen get various prizes and celebrate with 'winding up' speeches, sandwiches, cold chicken etc., and wash it down with cheap wine! I was very fortunate in winning a very acceptable prize in the form of a Roberts radio—absolutely ideal for our caravan. I was lucky to win a prize in the first place and even luckier that the prize was a wireless. I managed to get back home again by about 3 p.m. and, after a quick meal, resumed hard labour with the household packing routine.

This exercise went on until 2 a.m. Friday morning when I eventually persuaded Megan that the packing was complete and that she didn't really need to polish the floorboards! By this time we were both fairly exhausted and had moved into the caravan for eating and sleeping. I certainly didn't feel like embarking on a marathon run. I also detected a small swelling at the base of my tummy which I suspected might be a hernia. This was confirmed after we had completed our journey but fortunately it didn't give me a moment's worry or pain during the whole trip.

After a restless four hours sleep I woke at about 6 a.m. D-Day. Friday 18 May. I promptly wished I could go back to sleep again for about 100 days! Our first problem was to launch the car and caravan onto the road from our narrow entrance. Within five minutes I had turned this simple task into a nightmare! I didn't realise just how long a car and caravan were when linked together and that you actually had to think before turning too abruptly and remember that this monster behind was now part of the family! So, at precisely 6.15 a.m. I had blocked the main road out of Wincanton with the caravan not quite out of our entrance and the nose of the car within an inch of the far road wall. Fortunately this didn't inconvenience anyone other than a couple of early risers who were quite content to watch Megan and me disconnect and manhandle our heavy caravan. We couldn't work the reverse mechanism and didn't succeed to do so for the next 2,000-odd miles. When we eventually retrieved ourselves from this embarrassing situation there was a frosty silence as we headed for Wool. No doubt both Megan and I were wondering how we were going to cope on such a long journey if we couldn't even drive out of our entrance without getting into difficulties. I was pleased to think that I would be doing the running and Megan the driving!

We reached Wool, without further difficulties, at 11.30 a.m. Wool is in Dorset, five miles north of Lulworth Cove and a mile south of the river Frome. Ten miles to the west is the county town of Dorchester and twelve miles to the east lies Poole. Wool Bridge Manor can be found on the outskirts and near the banks of the river Frome. This is a fine seventeenth-century building, the seat of the

D'Urberville family, and made famous by Thomas Hardy's novel *Tess of the D'Urbervilles.*

I had a quick chat with Commander Nash who told me he had made arrangements for me to meet the Press at 2.30 p.m. as I entered Weymouth. This was our first meeting and I had no idea what his impressions were but I had the feeling he was eyeing me with that critical naval look that suggested that a couple of weeks in dry dock would do me a power of good! I just hoped I could manage to run as far as Weymouth! Then I remembered the Chinese proverb—'the longest journey starts with a single step'. I didn't mind the single step but I was concerned about the next four and a half million!

At exactly noon Commander Nash announced the start of my marathon run through his megaphone. He could just as easily have been starting the Henley Regatta. The crowd of puzzled onlookers outside Wool Post Office numbered about half a dozen—including two loyal helpers rattling their collecting boxes with unusual optimism! I set off at a smart pace hoping to escape this embarrassing scene, feeling tired, hungry and lonely. The past few hectic days had caught up with me and I had an outsize headache. I was beginning to wonder if I would ever see Wool again. To add to my misery I would now have to run almost non stop to Weymouth in order to arrive there at 2.30 p.m. and the distance was about 14 miles. As I had done very little running for the past three weeks we had planned to start by running five-mile stretches with a couple of hours rest in between. Now I wasn't even going to have time for lunch!

I caught up with Megan at a lay-by about five miles along the A352. It was where we had parked the caravan on our way in to Wool. I only had time to hitch on the caravan and have a quick drink of fruit juice and glucose and suggested to Megan that she set off after me at about 2 p.m. and try and park where the Press were supposed to meet me.

Soon after Owermoigne I turned off the A352 into the A353, through the village of Poxwell and towards the coast and the approaches to Weymouth. Soon after 2 p.m. Megan overtook me and a few minutes later Commander Nash sped by. I hoped he had left his megaphone in Wool!

As I joined the A354 main road from Dorchester, on the outskirts of Weymouth, I was feeling more exhausted and very thirsty, and as I struggled onwards I could see Commander Nash in the middle of the road armed with his megaphone. At least there was the prospect of a rest once I reached the caravan, which I could see parked a short distance ahead of the commander. As I approached I could see the Press man with his camera, which he brought into action as I trotted up to the scene.

Rest was not part of Commander Nash's schedule, and after a few dummy runs for the photographer's benefit and a visit from the police to move Megan off the two yellow lines, we were soon on the move again. Commander Nash, still armed with his megaphone, leapt into his car, ordering me to give him two minutes start. It took a lot of courage, following behind this naval officer, who was shouting my ambitions and hopes to thousands of holidaymakers lining the seafront of Weymouth. I was still hungry and almost too tired to run and yet I had to force myself to look relaxed, and it was a great effort to keep up with the commander's car. I cannot describe the relief I felt when we finally cleared Weymouth and I spotted Megan parked in a lay-by. At last we were to be left alone and I could eat and rest.

We still had quite a distance to travel before reaching our pre-selected camping site but at least we were well ahead of time. After a light meal of ham, salad and fruit I settled down for a well earned one and a half hour's rest. Just before 4 p.m. we set off on our last lap and after passing through Chickerell we turned off the B3157 at Langton Cross and headed for Langton Herring and Rodden. I was now free of the main traffic, no longer running under any pressure and was thoroughly enjoying this gentle jog through the English countryside. These roads were really too narrow for car and caravan but Megan had gone ahead of me so I wasn't too far behind if she ran into any difficulties.

Soon after 5 p.m. I could see the caravan parked on the grass verge about two miles ahead at the top of Chesters Hill. So the first day's run came to an end at 5.30 p.m. in a beautiful spot overlooking West Fleet and Chesil Bank. I had run just over 23 miles and felt very pleased but very tired.

After supper we walked over the fields and down to the beach. Merlin, our English springer spaniel, who had joined us on this venture was enjoying her first taste of freedom since early morning. In this tranquil and peaceful setting it was easy to relax and forget the tensions of the day. I drifted off to sleep with the faint sound of a fog horn somewhere on the coastline and the laughing call of a green woodpecker from the wood in the valley.

Sometime just before midnight I woke up feeling very sick and then spent the rest of the night either hanging over the hedge being sick, in the lavatory or trying to recover in bed. Most of that time was spent outside hanging over the hedge but luckily it was a lovely, warm, moonlit night. By the morning I was totally exhausted and the feeling of sickness was still with me. I couldn't keep any liquid or food in my stomach—I was immediately sick again, and also had a slight temperature. There was no possibility of running today. I felt so weak I could hardly stand. Megan decided to find a doctor, if only to prescribe some medication that would enable me to get back on the road at the earliest opportunity.

Just before noon Dr Rankin arrived and diagnosed my problem as some sort of food poisoning. He was charming and helpful and suggested a 48-hour rest would see me back to normal. He also left me some tablets to take to ease the sickness. It wasn't until late in the afternoon that I began to feel better and saw real prospects of a complete recovery. It gave me time to reflect of this seemingly disastrous start to my Round Britain Run. At this rate I envisaged completing the course sometime in December instead of August. I puzzled over the cause of the sickness and wondered if it was caused by the Thursday sales meeting with its stand up wine and buffet meal. Alternatively, the previous day I had run a lot further than I intended and probably hadn't eaten or drunk enough. It had been a hot, muggy day and I had felt under quite a lot of pressure. I believe this sort of tension does affect one's health. Perhaps this sickness was due, in part, to a degree of dehydration and I made a mental note to drink little and often for the remainder of my journey.

The following morning I was very delighted to feel no further signs of sickness and decided not to waste another day just sitting in the caravan. So, after a light breakfast, we left our campsite overlooking Chesil Bank. After a few hundred yards I discovered I wasn't quite as strong as I had thought. Anyway, it was downhill most of the way to Abbotsbury and another lovely day. I jogged along steadily and slowed to a walk every half mile so as not to get too exhausted. There was a wonderful view of the Abbotsbury Swannery on my left and I could see hundreds of swans and geese on the shoreline. Apparently swans have been bred there since 1393 to provide food for the local monastery.

As I entered the village I passed a fifteenth-century tithe barn which looked in excellent condition. If there had been sufficient time I would have visited the famous and beautiful 17-acre gardens of rare sub-tropical plants which lie to the west of the village.

Here in Abbotsbury we rejoined the B3157 and set off in the direction of Burton Bradstock. Being a Sunday there was very little traffic and it was particularly pleasant jogging along at a steady and relaxed pace. It was a cool, sunny day so we decided to have an early midday break and drove the caravan right down to the extreme westerly end of Chesil Bank at a place called Cogden. Our spaniel, Merlin, suddenly decided she was no longer frightened of the sea and, after a couple of attempts to cross the Channel, we decided to restrict her to a ball and chain!

From Cogden I decided to run a slight detour through West Bay, where I hoped to see a colleague, while Megan took the direct route through Bothenhampton. We had arranged to meet about a mile east of Chideock. I eventually found my friend, Mrs Shaun King, working in one of the beachfront sweet shops and, after we had exchanged surprised 'hellos' I was back on the road again. Megan didn't find a suitable lay-by and I eventually caught up with her parked by the side of the road in the town of Chideock. Unfortunately, she wasn't feeling very well and it seemed that she may have caught my sickness. So, instead of continuing my run I got into the car and we drove on to Charmouth where we booked into the Newlands Court Caravan Site.

By 8 p.m. she was so unwell that I phoned for a doctor who came out very promptly and gave her some tablets which helped her through the night. A disappointing end to what had been an enjoyable day. I had only covered 14 miles but it was more than I had thought possible when I first set off and I was feeling quite tired.

The next morning, Monday 21 May, started wet and miserable. Megan looked ill and exhausted but was game enough to get up about 11 a.m. and drove me back to the point in Chideock where I had abandoned my run the day before. I then ran the four miles to the caravan site where we had an early lunch before setting off again in a westerly direction.

We had planned that Megan should not risk the steep hills in and out of Lyme Regis so we agreed to meet at a small hamlet called Rousden. This was about a six-mile run for me and about 12 miles for Megan via Axminster. The hills in and out of Lyme Regis were particularly steep and impossible to run up. The woodlands were very beautiful with their spring foliage and the ground was carpeted with Bluebells—of which I am very fond. Apart from the occasional chiffchaff, there wasn't the same variety of birds that we had seen in the Chesil Bank area. There we had seen winchats, cuckoos and a whitethroat.

We met up at Rousden soon after 2 p.m. and after a drink and a short rest I set off for Seaton along a narrow coastal road while Megan continued on the A3052 towards Colyford, to the north of Seaton. We agreed to meet at the first lay-by after the intersection of the A3052 and my route out of Seaton and Beer. Fortunately there were no real problems although I tried to take a short cut from Beer and got a little lost. Eventually I spotted the caravan at about 6 p.m. I was feeling tired, hungry and surprisingly cold. I had run or jogged about eight miles since our last break but I felt it was too early to call a halt. I was beginning to worry that my daily average was too small.

After a quick tea we decided to camp at the Bowd Hotel which was about six miles further on. Commander Nash had apparently spoken to the proprietor who had agreed to us parking there over-night. I reached Bowd just after 8 p.m. and while Megan was cooking the supper I popped into the hotel and sank a few halves of shandy. I was beginning to drink a lot of liquid during the day but didn't seem to be eating any more than normal.

Since leaving Wool on 18 May I had now completed 61 miles in four days. Admittedly one day I had been ill and hadn't run at all and the first day was really a half day. Nevertheless, an average day's run of about 20 miles would see me completing my journey at Christmas on skis!

Once we got to the other side of Exeter I decided we would have to work harder. Get up earlier and go to bed later. The following morning both of us were feeling very much better and felt we had fully recovered from our sickness bout. Unfortunately the weather was not favourable as it was pouring with rain—like stair rods! It was too heavy and wet to attempt any running. We decided on an early lunch and were surprised to be joined by Commander Nash who was head-ing into Devon on Macmillan business. We agreed to keep in touch. I was already phoning him most evenings and giving him a progress report as he hoped to arrange a reception for us at Tavistock.

At 3 p.m. the rain had abated a little and I decided I must set off and clock up some mileage. I put on my expensive Nike showerproof clothing which I soon found afforded me no protection at all from the rain as I was soaked within ten minutes. Nevertheless, it did keep me warm and comfortable, particularly in Scotland, when I ran in frequent cold, misty and showery conditions. I soon discovered it was not quite so safe running in these conditions as the traffic doesn't always spot you until it is quite close. So it was necessary to concentrate 100 per cent and I had to step on the grass verge on several occasions. I always ran on the right hand side of the road unless the oncoming traffic was driving into a low setting or rising sun. On a dual carriageway I ran on the left hand side where often there was a white line giving an area of hard shoulder.

I finally caught up with Megan near Clyst St Mary at about 5 p.m. I was soaking wet, hungry and thirsty. So, after changing into warm clothing and enjoying several cups of hot tea and toast, we settled down to a long rest. We had decided not to attempt running through the city of Exeter until after the rush hour and we thought that would be about 6.30 p.m. I wanted to cross Dartmoor on the B3212 and arranged to meet Megan where this road crossed under the A30 to the west of Exeter. Fortunately there was so little traffic in the city centre that Megan was almost able to curb crawl and we kept in sight of each other until we reached the far side. I continued running until we reached Longdown by which time it was getting dusk and I was wet and too tired to go any further. I joined the caravan and we drove on for about four miles until we reached the edge of Dartmoor at Steps Bridge. We parked in the hotel car park and I was able to enjoy a couple of shandies before supper. It was nearly 40 years since my last visit to the Steps Bridge Hotel. I used to go there occasionally with my late brother when we lived about two miles away near Doccombe. My parents had bought a farm there just after the Second World War. I remember my mother travelling down overnight from Wales in a horsebox (on the train) and having to walk the pet Jersey cow about five miles from Christow station.

During the night we could hear the rain beating down on the caravan. I was feeling quite depressed as the daily average was not improving. I was hoping for a fine day to give us the chance of reaching the outskirts of Tavistock by the following night.

Wednesday morning started as another cold and drizzly day. After disconnecting the caravan we set off back to Longdown soon after 7 a.m. to the point where I had given up the night before. Megan returned to Steps Bridge to prepare breakfast, make the bed and replenish our water supplies etc. I found it very depressing having to start the day by running about four miles back to the point where we had spent the previous night. I decided that in future there would be no going back. Once we found our camping site I would complete my run to that point however late the hour.

Steps Bridge is the easterly gateway to Dartmoor Forest. The designation of Dartmoor as a National Park marked it out as one of Britain's finest landscape areas, a national asset whose unique and characteristic natural beauty must be protected and preserved for the enjoyment of the nation. Too few visitors to Dartmoor are aware that it is one of our best scenic areas and there are many monuments and relics from man's remote past to be found by the enthusiastic walker. The use of granite as a building material has allowed so many of Dartmoor's prehistoric monuments to survive. The moor is one of our granite masses or 'bosses' which forms the core of most of South West England. Much of the soil is peat of varying thickness but there are also light, gravelly soils. Among the distinctive features of the landscape is the 'tor' which is usually a mass of unrotted granite that has been left as a cap on a hill above the general level of the tableland.

It is also notorious for its fog which can develop rapidly. Much of it consists of low clouds which result from the rise of damp air over the western edge of the Moor. It is this westerly side—the Princetown and Tavistock area—that suffers most from these fogs and a heavier rainfall.

By the time I got back to the caravan the rain had stopped and there was even a suggestion of sunshine. I was feeling quite fit, fresh and looking forward to possibly my longest day's run. I wanted to cross Dartmoor in the one day. The previous evening I had telephoned Commander Nash and he told me that he had arranged for the Cancer Relief Committee at Tavistock to meet me at noon outside the Bedford Hotel. My sister had also arranged for the Press and a photographer to be present.

It was a steep climb out of Steps Bridge with oak woodlands on either side and masses of bluebells but the road was quite narrow and I suggested to Megan that she didn't stop again until she found a lay-by on the other side of Moretonhampstead.

After two miles I reached the small farm where my parents had lived. My father was a country solicitor and in 1944 he sold his practice in mid Wales in order to join the small boats supplying the Normandy invasion fleet. He joined up as a deckhand-cook for a period of about four months. After that he bought this smallholding in Devon. The land wasn't really very fertile as it consisted largely of granite rocks, woodlands and ferns. The cows were competing with the rabbits for what little grass existed! I sat on the stone wall opposite 'Rock Valley' farm and, while I rested, I remembered those happy days some forty years earlier when I had been waiting to join my first ship. During that period I worked quite hard on the farm with my father and elder brother, who had a serious heart complaint. My brother and I enjoyed the farm and spent many happy hours with the dog and our ferret. We used to make quite a lot of money from the rabbits we caught and I will never forget the wood pigeon I shot in our top wood which eventually fell, after 'towering' (when shot in the brain a bird will shoot skywards before dying), about a hundred yards away—straight in to my god daughter's pram! The feathers were flying in all directions. The baby was unhurt but the pigeon was quite dead.

In those days we had no 'mains' and pumped our water from a stream. Every morning we took turns on the hand pump. There was no electricity either so we used candles and Tilley lamps, and no telephone.

I was back on my feet within ten minutes heading for the little village of Doccombe and, as I ran through it, I started to climb up the hill again until I reached a crossroads about a mile beyond the village. From here I could look down on Moretonhampstead which was about a mile further on, but it was all downhill. When I reached Moretonhampstead I hoped I might see Megan as I knew we were short of groceries but there was no sign of her and with those narrow streets it would have been too difficult for her to park. In fact I had to run for a further three miles before I found her parked in a small lay-by. It was just after noon and I had completed about 12 miles. It was still a long way to Tavistock.

After a drink and a ten minute rest I changed into shorts for the first time for several days as it was getting quite warm and the sun was shining. We decided to meet for lunch at Two Bridges which was about ten miles further on. I was really enjoying this run as I was now becoming much fitter, the weather was sunny and the scenery beautiful.

It was quite a steep climb up to Moor Gate where it levelled off at about 1,400 feet. Then a gradual descent and a clear view to Warrenhouse Inn a couple of miles ahead. Half a mile before the inn I passed Bennetts Cross, a medieval granite guidepost on the wild track from Chagford to Tavistock. This road is quite open and narrow with most of the traffic travelling at a moderate speed—having regard for the ponies and sheep which wander across the road from time to time.

I was delighted to see that Megan had stopped at Postbridge where she took several photographs of me running over the famous Clapper Bridge, striding across the East Dart river with its colossal loose granite stones weighing up to eight tons each. It was an opportunity to enjoy an ice cream and lemonade and to reflect on this historic place, 1,400 feet above sea level, surrounded by prehistoric hut circles and groves dating back to the Stone Age.

Eventually I reached Two Bridges and found Megan parked near the West Dart river. We decided to have our late salad lunch on our deck chairs by the river. It was now quite hot and I felt in need of a good rest after lunch. I always took off my running shoes when I stopped for a break and changed into another pair. About twice a week I had to build up the worn outside heels with some special compound in a tube called 'Shoe-Goo'. It was excellent in stopping the wear on the heels.

It was a little after 4 p.m. when I set off up the hill from Two Bridges, branching off on to the B3357 road towards Tavistock. I had now covered about 20 miles and was beginning to tire but with only eight miles to the outskirts of Tavistock I walked slowly until I reached the crest of the hill and then set off at a gentle jog towards Rundlestone. I could now see the huge Dartmoor prison complex about a mile to my left. Its cold, grey, granite outline was a depressing sight even on a warm, sunny evening. Running freely across the countryside it was difficult not to feel some compassion for the inmates who were caged in that desolate building.

This great convict prison was built in 1806 to accommodate French and American prisoners taken during the Napoleonic War. It was closed when the war ended in 1815 but was reopened in 1850 as a convict prison and has since been considerably enlarged.

Rundlestone is just two miles from Two Bridges and from here the road begins to descend towards Merrivale and Tavistock (about six miles) in one direction and Princetown in the other direction. Megan was waiting at this junction and I stopped for a long drink of orange juice and glucose. I was now back on familiar ground as, last September, I had run in the Dartmoor Marathon and that course was from Tavistock to Rundlestone and on through Princetown. However, this time I would be running this six-mile stretch in the downhill direction. I had thoroughly enjoyed the Dartmoor Marathon and believe I was at my fittest to complete the ordeal in just under three and a half hours.

With Tavistock in sight and the route mainly downhill I set off on the last leg feeling less tired. Approaching Merrivale I ran off the road and onto the moor to look at the Bronze Age stone circle which is very close to the roadside. It's fascinating to stand and imagine that man lived and camped here nearly 4,000 years ago.

There was one last climb up from Merrivale and about another mile took me to the top of Pork Hill, just opposite Cox Tor, with a panoramic view across the moor and as far as Plymouth. At the bottom of Pork Hill we had arranged to park our caravan for two nights at Higher Longford Farm which was now a caravan site. I met Megan at the entrance to the farm and it took us about ten minutes to disconnect the caravan. Then I had a final mile to run to the outskirts of Tavistock. This we completed at about 6 p.m. and I was delighted to have achieved our objective and recorded our best score of 28 miles. We were able to avoid the town centre and took a short cut to Peter Tavey, collecting four trout from the trout farm, and reached my sister's home just before 7 p.m. After an excellent supper and a generous helping of wine I think I fell asleep before my head actually hit the pillow.

I felt quite pleased with myself as I was getting stronger and running further each day and we seemed to be able to cope with most of the problems. Tomorrow I would be 56 years old (or young!).

Thursday 24 May I awoke just after 8 a.m. feeling very, very stiff so I spent half an hour soaking in a hot bath. I don't know whether it was beneficial or not but it was a wonderfully relaxing feeling. I was due to meet the Press and the local Macmillan Cancer Relief committee at noon so I had timed my start from yesterday's finishing point at 11.50 a.m. It was only a short run of just over a mile and I had decided to cover the distance at quite a quick pace as I didn't want to look too fresh and spritely! As it turned out it was a very hot day and when I arrived at the Bedford Hotel I was already dripping with sweat and feeling uncomfortably stiff. After photographs and an amusing ten-minute chat with all concerned I set off through the town, past Sir Francis Drake's statue, and on to the A390 bound for Liskeard and Cornwall.

It was one of those lovely days when the sun is shining with the occasional large white cumulus clouds floating by. The hedges and

4 Macmillan Nurses supporters at Tavistock.

banks were coloured with bluebells, red campion and stitchwort and the yellow hammers were busily hunting the hedgerows.

By 1 p.m. I had climbed clear of Tavistock, walking up most of the steep hills, and was thankful to find Megan parked regularly with lemonade or fruit juice. She only had the car as we intended going back to my sister's for a second night. It was now becoming very hot and I discarded my running vest as I started to run down the very steep hill into Gunnislake. I was glad to reach the bottom and cross over the bridge into Cornwall as the steep downhill run had made my Bryant and May legs ache almost unbearably, both at the front and the back. This is a beautiful old bridge that links Devon to Cornwall (or, as the signpost says, Kernow) across the river Tamar.

It was a relief to walk up the steep hill out of the town. We managed to take a short cut by bypassing the main town centre of Callington, but the hilly route continued for several more miles. I was feeling quite tired and still very stiff, so I decided not to push my luck too far and eventually ended my day's run just before 4 p.m. and about three miles short of Liskeard.

We turned around and drove back to my sister's farm at Peter Tavey. I was convinced that another hot bath, birthday supper and an early night would be very acceptable and beneficial. Considering my stiffness the day's run of 17 miles wasn't too disappointing.

The following morning we said goodbye to my sister just after 9 a.m. and set off to Longford Farm at Moor Shop to collect our caravan. It took us nearly an hour before we reached last night's finishing point and already the skies were black and rain was imminent. It started to rain as I passed through Liskeard and the traffic was particularly busy, so I was thankful to catch up with Megan at East Taphouse and change out of my wet clothes before settling down to lunch. It remained a wet, cold and depressing day and I concentrated on keeping up a steady jogging pace. I felt less stiff and wanted to press on much later into the evening to make up for the late starts from the previous two or three days. I passed through Lostwithiel just before 4 o'clock and after a quick tea set off for St Austell which I entered at 6 p.m. I gave up after a further four miles feeling satisfied with the day's run of 27 miles.

We turned off the main road and found a suitable small lay-by near the village of Creed. We were beginning to sort out some of our minor problems such as collecting groceries and water and settling down to a fairly regular routine. I was now feeling stronger and fitter and my daily runs were approaching the 30-mile mark. In fact, I planned to set off an hour earlier tomorrow with the hope of camping that evening within ten miles of Lizard Point.

Once again, Saturday morning turned out to be wet and cold but at least I was making an earlier start at 7.30 a.m. After a couple of miles I stopped and bought a pint of milk, expecting Megan to catch me up in about ten minutes. It's surprising how heavy a pint of milk feels after running with it for about three miles. I cannot remember why Megan was so late, but we had words! I was inclined to get tense running on these sometimes narrow roads with heavy weekend traffic and pouring rain. From a safety angle it was necessary to be alert at all times as the driver's view of pedestrians is not so good through his windscreen wipers. Fortunately I ran through Truro before the busy lunch hour.

Truro is one of Cornwall's four Stannary or Coinage towns and is also known as the county's cathedral city.

I had to keep going for another four miles before locating Megan, parked just beyond Perranarworthal. I wasn't enjoying running in this wet, miserable weather but was now determined to complete my first 30-mile day. Just beyond Burnthouse I turned off the A394 and headed for Treverva and Gweek. Megan continued on the main road through Helston. We agreed to meet a couple of hours later at a place called Cross Lanes on the road to Lizard Point. It was a treat to leave the traffic of the main road and wander through the country lanes of Cornwall. It even stopped raining and the birds began to sing.

After Gweek I was running through woodland with young oaks and beeches, which were quite beautiful. The road was narrow but well surfaced and there was hardly any traffic. The woods were carpeted with moss, ferns and bluebells sweeping down to the little stream. In this area there were a lot of white bluebells. At Garras I had to stop for a break and someone kindly gave me two glasses of orange juice, which were very welcome. I reached the A3083 Lizard road just after 6 p.m. and met up with Megan at Cross Lanes as planned. We found a side road to park for the night and I was delighted with my run of 31 miles but worried because my right ankle had been a little painful for the last hour.

Sunday 27 May was sunny and I set off early for the six mile jog to Lizard Point. At 8.45 a.m. I passed close to the lighthouse, but continued further down the narrow road to the old lifeboat station. At 9 a.m. I had reached my first objective, the most southerly point of England, and had completed a distance of 188 miles in a few hours short of nine days—a daily average of just over 20 miles. I would have to aim to improve this considerably and was optimistic that this could be done. At best it was a start, and although there were still over 2,000 miles to run, I felt confident that we could manage it somehow.

7

Across Exmoor and South Wales

I rested for a while—sitting on a high bank looking out to sea, relaxing in the early morning sunshine and a gentle sea breeze. Hull down on the horizon was a tanker westward bound and I wondered for which port she might be heading. I remembered the last time I had seen Lizard Point was in the late 1950s. The weather conditions then were appalling. I was second mate on the SS *Clan Angus* and homeward bound from India with a cargo of jute, tea and hides. Our last port of call had been Lisbon and we had sailed on the evening tide. No sooner had we dropped the pilot when the weather began to deteriorate, with a severe westerly gale being forecast for the Bay of Biscay. November gales and the Atlantic Ocean can be an incompatible combination! When I came on watch at midnight it was blowing a full gale and we decided to alter course to a more northerly direction to take us further away from the lee coast. This also brought the ship's head more directly into those mountainous Atlantic rollers.

We were now clear of the shallower coastal waters, about a hundred miles south-west of Cape Finisterre, approaching the more exposed elements of the Bay of Biscay. Instead of rolling like a barrel we now corkscrewed from one mountaintop to the next and, with the ship so heavily laden, we were shipping some quite heavy seas. Although these wartime built 'Empire' ships were very under-powered, when loaded they were safe and stable. I never felt worried however severe the gale—although I would always prefer to run to the open ocean than coastal shelter.

We didn't see Cape Finisterre and we were navigating by dead reckoning. The sky remained heavily overcast, with driving rain. For the next two days the storm continued and there was no break in the cloud for sun or star sights. We had no modern aids such as radar or Decca Navigator and we steered by magnetic compass. Captain Cook would have been quite at home on the SS *Clan Angus*!

We struggled and wallowed across the Bay of Biscay with a course hopefully in the direction of Ushant. This is a lighthouse just to the west of Brest in northern France. In these conditions and without modern navigation aids it was like finding your way around in the dark. We had no idea how far the gale had blown us off course and the visibility was down to about half a mile at the most. To test our nerves it was necessary to sound the foghorn every two minutes under these conditions. We didn't see the Ushant light but continued on our north easterly course. I remember the relief when finally we sighted the characteristic group flashing light of Lizard Point at about 3 a.m. and were then able to establish our position before altering course more easterly and heading up the English Channel towards the pilot station off Dungeness.

The gale became ever more severe and we had further problems, but that's another story!

Anyway, it was interesting to reflect on earlier days and challenges but now I had rested and it was time to set off again in the direction of Land's End.

For the next seven or eight miles I was merely retracing my footsteps, but as soon as I reached Helston I was back on new territory. Helston is another of Cornwall's Stannary or Coinage towns and, in the Middle Ages, had been quite a busy port. In present times it is better known because of its proximity to the Royal Naval Air Station at nearby Culdrose. From this station many acts of bravery have been performed by air sea rescue teams operating from helicopters. My sister Frances had served in the WRNS at Culdrose in the 1950s.

The A394 took us along the coast road overlooking Mounts Bay and just after 3 p.m. I caught up with Megan in a lay-by just beyond Praa Sands. After tea and a short rest I set off with Megan to find a caravan site that we intended booking into for the next two days. We soon found the Wayfarers Camping Site at St Hilary and it didn't take us long to disconnect the caravan and return to the lay-by near Praa Sands.

I wanted to reach the outskirts of Penzance as a final target for the day. I had arranged with Commander Nash to run through the town centre at exactly 10 a.m. the following morning when there would be a group of Macmillan Cancer Relief Fund helpers to greet us. It was a lovely evening and I enjoyed the last seven- or eight-mile run which took me through Marazion where Megan and I had very nearly bought the post office when we had returned from New Zealand in

1979. It had such a lovely peaceful view looking out across the bay towards St Michael's Mount.

This little granite island rises to a 250 ft summit and is accessible by foot via a causeway at low tide or by boat from Marazion. Its splendid castle and priory, both founded by Edward the Confessor in the eleventh century, stand high above the small harbour.

It was about 7 p.m. as I ran past Penzance's helicopter terminal and I kept going for another half a mile before Megan picked me up. On our way back to the caravan we stopped at Marazion and thoroughly enjoyed an evening stroll along the beach while it was still warm and the sun was setting. I was looking forward to a hot shower which didn't materialise. I cannot think of anything more uncomfortable than a cold one!

Next morning it was about a six-mile drive from the caravan site to my starting point in Penzance. Megan had cut sandwiches, filled thermoses etc., as today we would only be using the car and rejoining the caravan later that evening after completing our visit to Land's End and starting on our easterly journey up Cornwall's northerly coast. I started my run at exactly 9.55 a.m. as I had calculated I would pass through the town centre a few minutes after 10 a.m. and hopefully the Macmillan Cancer Relief helpers would be on duty!

It wasn't wet, but nevertheless there was quite a cold north-westerly wind blowing and there were very few people to be seen. The Cancer Relief team were very conspicuous by their absence. We didn't see any of them although Megan had agreed to hang back and drive through about twenty minutes after me.

Penzance, the most westerly town in England, enjoys a mild climate all year round. The local gardens produce exceptional collections of magnolias, rhododendrons and other exotic shrubs. In fact, it was here that magnolias flowered for the first time in the British Isles.

At the small village of Catchall we had decided to take the southerly route on the B3283 to St Buryan, Polgigga and Land's End. We would return to Catchall on the A30 through Sennen and Crows-An-Wra.

I kept running throughout the morning and thought I had lost Megan at St Buryan. She had stopped to look at a delightful old church. This was quite wild countryside with very little traffic and I saw a pair of foxes in one of the fields of new potatoes. It was a lovely sunny day when we arrived at Land's End just before 12.30 p.m.

LANDS
END

NEW YORK 3147   JOHN O'GROATS 874

SCILLY IS   8
LONGSHIPS LI   SE 1½   COVENTRY 295
28 MAY 84

5 Arriving at Land's End.

This was our second objective. We were going to accept Land's End as our most westerly point but it was not terribly exciting as it came so soon after Lizard Point. So far we had completed 224 miles in ten days.

We enjoyed a long break, taking photographs, buying postcards, a snack lunch with ice cream and a well-earned rest. We had wonderful sea views of the Longships Lighthouse and further up the coast was the granite headland of Cape Cornwall with its natural beauty and prehistoric burial ground. It's always surprised me that the British mainland has only two capes—Cape Cornwall and Cape Wrath in Scotland.

The journey back to Penzance was uneventful but I couldn't help feeling disappointed that I hadn't set off earlier in the morning, which I would have done had I known we were not going to be met in Penzance. For late May it was surprisingly cold but at least the breeze was behind me as I headed towards Hayle and Redruth along the A30.

We called it a day at Cannons Town and we returned to the caravan site for a second night. I refused another cold shower! I telephoned Commander Nash and arranged to enter Newquay at 10 a.m. in two days time—Wednesday 30 May.

Tuesday 29 May was a much sunnier day although the cold breeze seemed to persist. After a good breakfast we left the campsite soon after 9 and I was back jogging along the A30 at 9.30. I was now running fairly consistently around 30 miles a day and we had worked out a regular routine which divided the day into running about 15 miles before lunch and the second 15 miles between 2 and about 7. We used a clipboard with a new piece of scrap paper for each day. Whenever I left the caravan I noted the exact time and the exact mileage on the car. This we reset at the end of each day. On the back of the clipboard I had written the following standard information for Megan to refer to:

Mile Times

Fast and downhill	8 minutes
Average and level roads	9 minutes
Hilly and windy conditions	12 minutes
Walking only	16 minutes

From this table, my departure time, weather conditions, type of country and the mileometer reading Megan was always able to guess fairly accurately when and where to expect me. On many occasions she would stay on in the caravan after I had left although I much preferred her to be ahead of me so I was always in the position of running towards her and not away from her. Then I didn't have to worry whether or not the car would start or whether she had a flat tyre etc. With very little else to think about I was inclined to worry or become agitated if Megan didn't overtake me within about half an hour of my own departure. Once she was ahead of me I rarely worried, even if it took me a couple of hours to make contact again.

It didn't take very long before I reached Hayle and there appeared to be a large number of holidaymakers busy with their early morning shopping. It was a change to get back onto a dual carriageway, as I did soon after leaving the town, which is usually the safest place to run. I then ran on the left hand side of the road where generally there is a thick, white line giving about 18 inches of road space between that line and the hedge. The one disadvantage is that traffic will be passing much closer and at very fast speeds, but very rarely will a car or lorry transgress onto that white line. However, it can make your nerves jangle if there are too many of the heavy juggernauts overtaking as they tend to blow you towards the ditch or suck you towards them. The problem is that you never know which it is going to be!

The sides of the roads of Britain are littered with nuts, bolts, sparking plugs, bits of wire, coins, hub caps and short bits of ropes from lorries. I always keep half an eye on where my footsteps are falling as it could be too easy to twist an ankle. If I'd pushed a wheelbarrow ahead of me I could have filled it at least ten times! (It didn't take long before I picked up a spare hub cap for our Ford Sierra!)

I used to worry about the overtaking heavy lorries with their dangling bits of rope. I rarely looked back at traffic while I was running and I fortunately do not recall being touched by flapping canvas or rope from a passing vehicle.

The new dual carriageway took us clear of Camborne and Redruth. I had joined Megan in a lay-by near Redruth. We then drove into the town to purchase a new three-pin plug for the car–caravan lighting connection. This shortened my dinner time as it took us nearly an hour to find the caravan shop, get back to the lay-by and then another half hour to fix on the new connection. This was part of the running repairs we would need to do from time to time as the journey progressed.

It got quite boring on the dual carriageway as there was little of interest in the way of hedgerow plants or birds although, just before turning off the A30 on to the A3075 for Newquay, I saw a single cowslip! In my youth we used to see fields of them but now, I understand, the plant is an endangered species.

We were back on the narrower, busy Cornish roads and I was running on the right hand side of the road towards the on-coming traffic. By the time we reached Newquay my right leg was tingling with nettle stings where I had needed to get too close into the hedge on several occasions. I had also decided to take out a single, straightforward £25,000 accident-only insurance policy. I also wondered what country we were in as we passed through the villages of Perranzabuloe, Goonhavern and Rejerrah! It sounded more like Germany or India.

I actually stopped running just before we entered Newquay but it was about four miles the other side that we found our camping site for the night. It was down a side road and seemed adjacent to a big estate. I didn't dare let Merlin loose in the woods. It was full of lovely old oaks, beech, sycamore, rhododendron, yews and probably pheasants too! In fact, when I strolled along the edge of the wood later in the evening, with Merlin on a lead, I could hear a number of cock pheasants calling and also spotted a little goldcrest in a yew tree.

On Wednesday 30 May we had to retrace our footsteps to where I had completed my previous day's run. This was always a nuisance because it meant disconnecting the caravan and it had that psychological effect of feeling that it was necessary to complete 'x' miles before making a start for today's total. Anyway, we had an extra hour in bed before setting off back to the southerly side of Newquay. Once again I timed my run into the town centre for 10 a.m. and once again there was disappointment and no evidence of the Macmillan Cancer Relief local committee. When I had cleared the centre I turned around and ran back into the town—straight down the middle of the road—hoping someone might call out. It was nearly 10.30 a.m. before I gave up and headed off in the direction of St Columb Major, where I would rejoin the A39.

Before reaching that point it was quite a steep climb out of Newquay and about three miles to where we'd left the caravan. When I reached the caravan I was feeling a little angry that we hadn't been met in Newquay and that I had therefore wasted several hours running time. Megan didn't turn up for another hour, which didn't improve my temper! Although I had a spare key for the caravan so I could get refreshments and rest I couldn't run on as it was too difficult for Megan to hitch the caravan on to the car. I think it was one of those occasions where she had been enjoying a shopping spree and had completely forgotten how late it was. I confess that I tended to be somewhat irritable if Megan wasn't where I expected her to be, and at the right time.

It's an odd, helpless and lonely feeling to be standing in the middle of a strange city street, in shorts and singlet, wondering whether your wife and mobile home are ten miles ahead or ten miles astern! The feelings are no different if you are on the top of Shap Fell, in pouring rain, pondering the same problem. That's my excuse for being a little edgy at times! By the time Megan turned up it was well after noon but at least she'd brought a choc ice which was very acceptable!

After hitching on the caravan and deciding we would have a late lunch I set off with the intention of meeting Megan in a lay-by a few miles south of Wadebridge. It was sunny but quite cold. It wasn't a difficult road to run on but I was finding it very tiring trying to maintain a steady rhythm. There seemed to be so many interruptions, such as heavy traffic, with overtaking vehicles, distractions in the villages, hills etc. It was a different type of running from what I was used to. At home I could pick my quiet country road and set off on a 10- or 15-mile run knowing there would be no interruptions at all.

I found Megan just about where I had expected her—just beyond a signpost to St Jidgey. We didn't stay very long and it was a warmer evening when, at about 5 p.m. I ran through Wadebridge. One of the finest medieval bridges in England can be seen there. It spans the river Camel. Built in 1485 and widened in 1849, it is 320 feet long with 17 arches. It is thought that packs of wool may have been sunk into the riverbed to make firm bases for the piers.

Two miles south west of Wadebridge lies the tiny village or hamlet of St Breoke, where you will find a surprisingly large and quite beautiful church.

My great-great-great-great-grandfather, the Revd Carolus Pole, was rector of St Breoke from 1710 to 1730. His daughter-in-law was Anne Buller, granddaughter of Bishop Jonathan Trelawney who was committed to the Tower of London and charged, with six other bishops, with sedition. They were found not guilty by a jury and James II fled to France! Carolus was the son of Sir John Pole Bt of Shute.

There was surprisingly little traffic as I ran on northwards towards St Kew Highway and I eventually spotted Megan on the outskirts of Camelford. I joined the car and we drove on through the town and found an ideal camping spot 1½ miles on the other side. After disconnecting the caravan Megan drove me back to where I had stopped running and while I was completing that last couple of miles she was back at base waiting for me and cooking supper. This was the pattern we were to follow for the rest of the venture—with a few exceptions.

Thursday morning, the last day of May. I was up a little earlier. It was 7 a.m. and I decided to leave Megan in bed and clock up a few miles before breakfast. I did have a small bowl of cornflakes and a cup of milk before setting off. There was nothing for me to do as we always slept with the caravan already connected. Megan only had to let off the caravan handbrake before setting off after me and there wasn't the problem of going back to the previous night's stopping point.

I was now running between Bodmin Moor and the sea. The mornings were still surprisingly chilly and I found it too cold for shorts.

Megan overtook me at about 8 a.m. and I shouted for her to stop at the next lay-by for breakfast. I felt quite pleased to have notched up over six miles already. The next session was longer and took me through Stratton, thus avoiding the coastal town of Bude. At least I could smell the salt air! There's plenty of history in this area. Sir Bevil Grenville used the Tree Inn as his headquarters (it was then a manor house not an inn) before leading his Cavaliers to victory in the Civil War in 1643. The battleground was just north of the village at Stamford Hill.

A couple of miles north of Stratton I took a short cut over a very steep hill and on a narrow road. It saved about a mile before bringing me back onto the A39 again. It was drizzling and very heavily overcast as I approached Kilkhampton. Megan was parked outside the church, which she persuaded me to visit. It was very interesting with its beautifully carved bench ends, a splendid barrel roof and an elaborately carved Norman doorway. The church itself dates from between the twelfth and fifteenth centuries. We didn't stay too long as Megan was keen to visit Clovelly later in the afternoon.

Although it continued to threaten rain and the heavy dark clouds remained, I managed to keep up quite a good pace and felt less tired than yesterday. It was soon after 4 p.m. that I passed the crossroads marking Welcombe to the west and Meddon to the east. I was now back in Devon and running on the edge of the National Park area of outstanding natural beauty that stretches from Bude to Hartland Point and then on round the coast to Westward Ho!, Ilfracombe and Exmoor. Unfortunately, it remained heavily overcast and a downpour of rain seemed inevitable.

I had another three or four miles to go before I eventually saw Megan waiting by a garage opposite the B3237 which leads down towards Clovelly. The garage owner very kindly allowed us to disconnect and park our caravan—we didn't dare risk driving it down to the Clovelly car park.

I wasn't considering Clovelly as part of my run, which was a wise decision considering the steepness of the approaches. The car park is still a long way from the fishing village. No cars are allowed there because the steep cobbled street, lined with lovely old houses, descends 400 feet to the sea in a series of steps. Donkeys are used to transport visitors' luggage and zig-zag steps allow pedestrian access down the wooded cliffs to the tiny quay and a pebble beach. It's an incredible place and must rank as one of the loveliest corners of

England. Clovelly Court, the great house, stands, with the church, high above the village and the sea. With its magnificent views it has 600 years of memories and history. The fifteenth-century church is approached through an avenue of yews. Its doorway has Norman stones in it and the font is older still. Charles Kingsley, author of *Westward Ho!*, spent his youth in Clovelly. His father was rector of the parish for a number of years.

Rector Kingsley was popular for he was 'a man who feared no danger, and could steer a boat, hoist and lower a sail, shoot a herring net and haul a seine as one of themselves'. When the herring fleet put out to sea the he and his wife and boys would go down to the quay for a parting service and all would join in saying the 121st Psalm.

It was a wonderful break, but quite an exhausting exercise to climb back up from the beach to the car park. However, after a cup of tea, toast and a piece of cake I was ready to set off once again after we had reconnected our caravan and thanked the garage proprietor for free caravan parking.

Megan found a quiet camping spot down a side road just beyond Buck Cross so my final session was only five miles, but it gave me my best day's run of 36 miles. So perhaps I was entitled to feel a little exhausted climbing up from the Clovelly beach as, at that stage, I had already completed 30 miles for the day.

I always enjoyed my supper, which was usually a cooked one of fish or chicken. We would often go to bed early so that I could relax more easily and we could read, write or listen to the wireless.

The blisters on my feet, that I had been worried about a couple of days ago, seemed to be clearing up without any further medication. I changed my shoes about five times a day, in fact after each running session, but I confess I didn't actually wash my feet too often and could only afford to change my socks once a day. We couldn't otherwise keep up with the washing.

Soon after supper the heavens opened and the rain was like drum beats on the caravan roof until I eventually fell asleep.

The first day of June found me on the road by 7 a.m. and jogging through the picturesque town of Bideford at 8 a.m. I ran over the beautiful fifteenth-century bridge which spans the river Torridge and counted 22 arches, but I must have missed two as the correct count is 24. To take modern traffic the bridge has been considerably renovated and widened.

Between 1550 and 1750 Bideford was the principal port of north

Devon and the home of a renowned shipbuilding industry. Sir Richard Grenville, who obtained a charter for the town from Queen Elizabeth I, crewed his ship *Revenge* entirely with Bideford men. The brave little vessel will always be famous for its stand against 15 Spanish ships at Flores in the Azores. It had carried Drake's flag against the Armada and, although she was now hit by 800 cannon balls and most of her crew had been killed, it was a storm soon after the battle that finally saved her.

The Revenge: A Ballad of the Fleet

Then spake Sir Richard Grenville: 'I know you are no coward;
You fly them for a moment to fight with them again.
But I've ninety men and more that are lying sick ashore.
I should count myself the coward if I left them, my Lord
    Howard,
To those Inquisition dogs and the devildoms of Spain.
So Lord Howard passed away with five ships of war that day,
Till he melted like a cloud in the silent summer heaven;
But Sir Richard bore in hand all his sick men from the land
Very carefully and slow,
Men of Bideford in Devon.
And we laid them on the ballast down below;
For we brought them all aboard,
And they blest him in their pain, that they were not left to
    Spain,
To the thumbscrew and the stake, for the glory of the Lord.

He had only a hundred seamen to work the ship and to fight,
And he sailed away from Flores till the Spaniard came in sight,
With his huge sea-castles heaving upon the weather bow.
'Shall we fight or shall we fly?
Good Sir Richard, tell us now,
For to fight is but to die!
There'll be little of us left by the time the sun be set.'
And Sir Richard said again: 'We be all good English men,
Let us bang these dogs of Seville, the children of the devil,
For I never turned my back on Don or devil yet.'

And the gunner said 'Ay ay', but the seamen made reply:

'We have children, we have wives,
And the Lord hath spared our lives.
We will make the Spaniard a promise, if we yield, to let us go;
We shall live to fight again and to strike another blow.'
And the lion there lay dying, and they yielded to the foe.

And the stately Spanish men to their flagship bore him then,
Where they laid him by the mast, old Sir Richard caught at last,
And they praised him to his face with their courtly foreign
    grace.
But he rose upon their decks and he cried:
'I have fought for Queen and Faith like a valiant man and true.
I have only done my duty as a man is bound to do.
With a joyful spirit I, Sir Richard Grenville, die!'
And he fell upon their decks and he died.

Alfred, Lord Tennyson

As I headed for Instow and Barnstaple I kept looking back at this
elegant bridge which dominates the centre of Bideford.

It had all the makings of a lovely sunny day and it showed off the
beautiful colourings of the sailing dinghies, all of different sizes and
shapes, anchored in the estuary off Instow. On the other side of the
estuary is Westward Ho!, and also the small but thriving ship building
yards of Appledore.

We stopped for breakfast just beyond Instow and here we had a
clear view across Bideford Bay to Lundy Island. We each had a pair
of binoculars which we found very useful during our journey, particularly for identifying birds.

After breakfast we agreed to meet next at the first available lay-by
after Barnstaple. I was then going to take a short cut over a narrow
and steep road into the western approaches of Exmoor. Megan would
have to tow the caravan along the main A39 to Blackmoor Gate
before turning east on the secondary road in the direction of
Simonsbath and Exford. We agreed to meet at Challacombe. This way
I hoped to save about four miles.

By 11 a.m. I had reached the outskirts of Barnstaple and was
surprised at how much the town had grown. In fact, I took a wrong
turning and had to ask directions. I'd spent a couple of months in
hospital here many years ago but I didn't remember it at all.

It appears to be another old and attractive port, like Bideford, with a history of trade and shipbuilding. Barnstaple too has a very old bridge spanning the river Taw.

Megan had navigated successfully through the town and we met just on the northern outskirts. After an early lunch we set off in our different directions and I had optimistically told Megan I hoped to reach Challacombe by 2 p.m., allowing 1½ hours for my ten-mile short cut.

As soon as I left the main road the countryside was quite wild but very peaceful. Hardly a car passed me as I headed for Bratton Fleming. It was becoming very, very warm and I stopped at a couple of isolated cottages for a glass of water. After about two miles it was too tiring to run and it seemed to be a continuous uphill trek. I thought it would never end—but the scenery was marvellous.

When I eventually reached Bratton Fleming I bought a bar of chocolate and a pint of milk and I carried these for a further half a mile until I had reached the top of the world. It was a magnificent view from 700 feet. I sat down and rested and surveyed this wonderful scene across fields and villages to the sea. I could see Ilfracombe, Barnstaple and across the beautiful blue sea—that seemed to be at my feet—was Lundy Island. As I sat on a bank drinking in the view the only sound was a skylark and the distant bleating of sheep. It reminded me of some verses of that lovely poem we learned as children—*All Things Bright and Beautiful*:

> Each little flower that opens
> Each little bird that sings
> He made their glowing colours
> He made their tiny wings.
>
> The purple headed mountain
> The river running by
> The sunset and the morning
> That brightens up the sky.
>
> The cold wind in the winter
> The pleasant summer sun
> The ripe fruits in the garden
> He made them every one.

He gave us eyes to see them
And lips that we might tell
How great is God Almighty
Who has made all things well.

Chorus:
All things bright and beautiful
All creatures great and small
All things wise and wonderful
The Lord God made them all.

Already I was running (or rather walking) about half an hour behind schedule and when the downhill part came it was just too steep to run. Finally I arrived at Challacombe but an hour later than I had intended. There was no sign of Megan but, as agreed, I set off along the new route towards Simonsbath. Immediately, I encountered a steep hill which took 20 minutes before reaching a corner near the top where Megan was parked in a small lay-by. I was quite ready for a large pot of tea, a good supply of toast with jam and 'feet up' for a couple of hours!

We were now in the Exmoor Forest National Park. When so much of 'England's green and pleasant land' has been marred by urban spread this is another corner of our country that remains a priceless heritage for the enjoyment of all. The 43,500 acres of open moorland is divided between extensive sheep grazing lands, with heather dominant on Dunkery, Winsford Hill and Withypool Common, and large areas of conifer plantations. Nor must we forget the tough and wild little Exmoor pony that has roamed these moors for hundreds of years. Almost the whole of Exmoor is composed of Devonian and Old Red Sandstone rocks. Climatic conditions are mild and I feel that this moor is warmer and softer than its granite neighbour, Dartmoor. Historically, like Dartmoor, our Bronze Age ancestors were here and so were the Romans. Hill forts and barrows can be seen encircling the tops of the steep hills and the Romans had two signal stations on the northern coast to keep an eye on the restless Welsh across the Severn estuary.

It was nearly 5 p.m. when I set off towards Simonsbath and, strangely, I didn't feel at all tired. Perhaps it was this wonderful scenery and the warmth of the sunshine. After a couple of miles I had crossed into Somerset and, as I approached Simonsbath, I was looking down on the Barle, surely one of Exmoor's most attractive rivers, which, further downstream, is spanned by the most famous clapper bridge at Tarr Steps. At one point I was enjoying the scenery so much that an on-coming vehicle decided to wake me up with an angry blast on his horn as he swept by. It gave me quite a fright and I stumbled into the hedge and was severely stung by nettles. Not a particularly considerate motorist but probably I had strayed too far into the road and wasn't concentrating as much as I should have done. These warnings are useful and one is careful not to repeat these sorts of mistakes.

Megan was waiting in the centre of Simonsbath armed with an ice cream. I had only completed four miles since my last stop so I enjoyed my refreshment walking up the hill where I reached a point 1,100 feet above sea level en route for our final stop at Exford. This final six miles took me just over an hour of steady running and it was about 6.30 p.m. as I ran down the last hill into this well kept Exe Valley village. Hunting and horses are its bread and butter and the Devon and Somerset Stag Hounds are based here. What a peaceful and pretty little village—but I wondered what it was like in winter.

Finding a spot to park overnight was surprisingly difficult but we eventually found one about a mile to the north near Edgcott, close to the river Exe. The days' total was another 36 miles.

Saturday 2 June was sunny again and I was up and running before 8 a.m. Or rather walking as, for 'starters', it's almost a two-mile uphill climb out of Exford on the road to Dunster. There was yet another steep hill on either side of Luckwell Bridge and we stopped for breakfast just before Wheddon Cross.

Again, the scenery was marvellous and the steep woodlands of wild oak and beech either side of the valley were full of bird life and song. However, as we approached Timberscombe, along the A396, these changed to plantations of Forestry Commission firs and one could see the differing scenery as we approached Dunster and the coast where Exmoor merges into the Brendon Hills and the landscape changes from wild heathland to a tapestry of fields and forest.

Soon after 11 a.m. I threaded my way through this beautiful medieval village dominated by its romantic castle. Its unspoilt condition is largely due to its constant ownership by the Luttrell family for some 600 years until 1950.

As soon as I ran onto the A39 (Minehead to Bridgwater) road the running conditions altered and there was rich pasture and arable land with winter cereals and crops of new potatoes. The soil was red and rich. No poor farmers here!

This is not a wide road and on Saturday 2 June it was fairly busy. It was not possible, under these conditions, to maintain a steady pace, as frequently I had either to stop or walk as it was too dangerous to do otherwise. It was frustrating but I just had to progress in the best possible way. Megan had planned to leave the caravan about seven miles further on, disconnect it and dash into Taunton to collect our daughter Nicola to join us for the rest of the day's running. Apart from the heavy traffic it was quite an easy jog through Washford and Williton but then I began to climb up to West Quantoxhead where, again, there were some wonderful views across the Bristol Channel of Barry and Cardiff. The islands of Flat Holm and Steep Holm were also clearly visible.

West Quantoxhead is on the northern edge of the Quantocks and just a mile from the sea, but it was a little farther on that I found the caravan parked in an awkward, sloping lay-by. I had my lunch of salad, fruit and a glass of milk, then settled down for an hour's rest.

I left the caravan after 3 p.m., having noted my departure time for Megan, but I was a little concerned in case they had difficulty in reconnecting the caravan. I hoped, if they found it difficult, that they would just come and collect me and not do anything foolish. I had visions of the caravan rolling down the hill out of control. I was relieved, at about 4 p.m., to see Megan and Nicola wave as they over-took me. They then parked almost round the next corner and I took advantage of another rest and another ice cream. Megan found a place to park for the night behind the Malt Shovel Inn at Cannington but I continued my run into the centre of Bridgwater. It was here that Megan collected me and we then went back to Nicola's home in Taunton where I lay in a lovely hot bath for about an hour before sitting down to an excellent supper. The third successive day to clock up 36 miles.

It poured with rain most of Saturday night but we were fortunate to start Sunday in reasonable conditions. We breakfasted after five miles and, at this point, it did rain heavily but I managed to make steady progress along the A38 towards Bristol. I hoped to reach the Downs in Bristol before 7 p.m.

We had arranged to meet the Cancer Relief Committee and the Press on the following morning. Soon after breakfast our course took us more inland and it was quite a climb up to the villages of

Winscombe and Churchill which lie on the edge of the Mendips. Fortunately, there was very little traffic and running conditions were good. In fact, towards evening, the weather became warm and sunny. It was quite an uneventful day. I joined Megan on the outskirts of Bristol and we then drove under the suspension bridge where we found a suitable lay-by and disconnected the caravan. It was then easy for Megan to take me back to the outskirts and complete my run into Bristol. However, just before the suspension bridge I turned off towards Bristol Zoo and up onto the Downs where Megan was wait-ing. We then went back to the caravan, reconnected it and drove on slowly to the camping site at Severn Beach (Villa Park Camping Ground).

It was important to memorise this route as I would be running along it tomorrow.

After we had docked for the night I telephoned my niece Elizabeth in London and she told me that tomorrow's meeting on the Downs had been cancelled. I then rang the local Press and they were interested in sending out a reporter who would contact me near the water tower at 10 a.m.

Monday 4 June was not going to be my best day! The reporter did not turn up and I waited patiently (or, probably, impatiently) until 11 a.m. and then set off on the ten-mile run back to the caravan at Severn Beach.

It was also easier for Megan to keep me in view as she was only driving the car and not towing. It took me 1½ hours, no stops, to complete this stage of the journey. After a quick change into sports jacket and trousers we raced back in the car to Bristol to meet Nicola for lunch. At that time Nicola was working in the city centre. It was a quick lunch as I got lost in the city traffic and had difficulty finding a car park!

It was 4.30 p.m. before I was back in shorts and heading for the Severn Bridge. Knowing I couldn't run over the bridge, Megan went ahead looking for a suitable lay-by about two miles from the motor-way roundabout where she would pick me up. I didn't enjoy this spell of running. For some reason I was worried by the heavy traffic and felt very vulnerable to the dangers. There was no hard shoulder for me to run on and I felt very relieved when I spotted Megan ahead of me. We must have been nearly three miles from the bridge but I was happy to be driven from this point.

I intended starting again from the first roundabout on the A48 on the Chepstow side. When we crossed the bridge Megan (on my instructions!) took the wrong turn and we found ourselves on the M4 bound for Newport! In fact, we had to drive almost into Newport before being able to turn off and head back eastwards along the A48 to Chepstow. However, we had dropped off the caravan on the A48 about five miles east of Newport so at about 6 p.m. I started off on my second and final spell for the day—but with only ten miles to my credit. I was feeling depressed and, for the first time, wondered whether I should give up. The speed and dangers of the heavy traffic between Bristol and the Severn Bridge had frightened me.

Life can be odd at times. This second session of mine was run under possibly the safest conditions of the whole journey. It was only a seven-mile stretch but most of it had either pavement or cycle path. Although the day ended with only a 17-mile total I was no longer depressed and determined that I could now carry on and succeed, provided I remained free from injuries.

This Severn Bridge, the Dartford Tunnel and a particular problem near Port Talbot were the only three sections of the whole route that I didn't actually run on. The other exception was the Kylesku Ferry linking Unapool and Kylestrome in north west Scotland—and I certainly wasn't going to swim it!

It was just as well I fell asleep that night with renewed confidence because it was going to be a testing day. Knowing we were running through two large cities I was up early and pounding the pavement in heavy rain soon after 6.30 a.m.

We got through Newport without any problems but it was still early in the morning and we had avoided the rush hour. I did have one narrow squeak on the outskirts when I stepped off the pavement to avoid a puddle and was bumped gently on the shoulder by an overtaking postal van. Normally I might have heard the vehicle but, with the rain, I had my hood up.

We breakfasted in a lay-by near Castleton, midway between Newport and Cardiff. We had a problem—lack of dry, clean running gear, so this time I didn't bother to change at all—except for my running shoes. Megan was trying her best to dry clothing with our car heater. Washing them was not possible.

I didn't feel too disheartened as I set off again in the direction of Cardiff at 11 a.m. It was still pouring with rain but I was determined to keep up the daily average and, furthermore, the rain looked set in for the day.

I hadn't been to Cardiff since 1955 when I had passed my Board of Trade Masters' Certificate but I knew the city would have changed considerably since that date. I was delighted to enter the outskirts via Newport Road and, when I was opposite number 126, I couldn't resist ringing the doorbell. The astonished manageress of the youth hostel invited me in when I explained that my father was born in the house nearly one hundred years ago. She must have thought I was completely mad, dressed in running shorts, vest and shoes with the rain pouring off me. She seemed delighted to show me around the property and wished me all the best as I took my leave and plodded off into the rain and the city centre. That quick five-minute break had cheered me up no end!

All the signs seemed different from what I had expected and I began to worry when or if I'd ever catch up with Megan. I didn't dare stop as I knew I would soon become chilled. We had planned on making for Barry and then along the coast road to Bridgend. As I was emerging on the western side of Cardiff an incident occurred that I won't forget for a long time. I was approaching a roundabout in an anti-clockwise direction when I noticed a heavy lorry thundering down the hill towards me. I was quite safe on the edge of the pavement with my head down against the driving rain. At the last moment I realised the danger—as this juggernaut was almost alongside me—the road drains were blocked and there was a 6-inch river alongside me. As this 30 ton, 16-wheeled monster hit the flood I could see this huge column of water rising from the road. It hit me in the face and neck with such force it nearly knocked me over. About ten gallons of water went straight down my neck and then divided at a very sensitive point with five gallons shooting down each leg! If I close my eyes I can still see myself—like a frozen TV shot—with both feet in the air, water pouring out from each leg and shaking a frustrated fist at the unfortunate driver. I hope at least that he got a laugh out of it as he certainly couldn't have avoided it.

I really was in trouble now if I didn't find warmth soon and I thought it very likely that Megan might have got lost. It was now nearly 12.30 p.m. and I had run about ten miles since breakfast. I kept my eyes open for a police car, which I intended to stop, but decided to carry on for about two more miles before telephoning the local police station.

It was all a built-up area and completely devoid of any sensible lay-bys but, just as I was running into Barry, I saw Megan parked in

6 Viewing my grandparents' grave at Llanmaes in the Vale of Glamorgan.

a bus stop.

There's not much room in a caravan for two people, a dog and wet clothing!

Two plates of hot soup and I was back to normal and delighted to have completed 20 miles before lunch for the first time.

Later in the afternoon the weather cleared and we had quite gentle and easy runs past Cardiff Airport, St Athan and finally the little village of Llanmaes. Here we parked for the night in a side road and, after supper, I visited the village church of St Catwg. My maternal grandfather, the Revd Daniel Evans, was rector of this parish for 38 years and it was my mother's birthplace. On the north wall of this small but ancient church is a very old painting of St George rescuing the princess from the dragon at the gate of the castle. It was my mother who discovered this when, as a teenager, she had been asked by her father to wash the north wall. The parish register is the oldest in the Vale of Glamorgan, dating from 1583. It contains some interesting entries, including the burial of Ivan Yorath, a native of Llantwit Major, who was buried on Saturday 17 July 1621 at the ripe old age of 180. He was a soldier at the battle of Bosworth Field and, to quote the entry, 'lived much by fishing'.

The church silver plate includes an Elizabethan chalice hallmarked 1569. The paten is pre-Reformation and dated 1459.

We left Llanmaes very early—soon after the 6 a.m. news—which reminded us that it was 6 June and the 40th anniversary of D-Day. I remember it very clearly as I was at school in Kent and we seemed to be in the direct path of the thousands of aircraft that droned overhead throughout the night on their deadly missions to the battle beaches. When we got up at dawn we could see this endless stream of aircraft unchallenged in their supremacy of the skies.

Back to the running! It was a lovely sunny morning as I headed off in the direction of Bridgend and I wished I had more time to take the coastal route through St Donats and Marcross where my parents used to spend their summer holidays. Nevertheless, from this more northerly road I still had a wonderful view back across the Bristol Channel and a clear sighting of Minehead and Dunkery Beacon on Exmoor. It was only four days ago that we were looking in the opposite direction.

We had two fairly easy running sessions in the morning but suddenly things got difficult as we approached Port Talbot. Somewhere near the giant Margam steelworks there were huge road diversions and alterations. There were large signs diverting traffic onto the motorway—where, of course, I was restricted from running—and another sign prohibiting pedestrians on the A48 route.

I told Megan to take the motorway route and, just as I was climbing over the A48 pedestrian barricade, a police car flashed by waving a warning hand at me. I ran after Megan who, having seen the incident, had pulled into the side and was waiting for me. I had no option but to take a lift of a couple of miles along this motorway diversion before it rejoined the A48.

We stopped in a narrow lay-by for a quick lunch and the caravan rocked each time a huge lorry passed. It was terribly hot and I was drinking large quantities of orange juice and lemonade.

We rejoined the A48 which took us to the northern outskirts of Swansea. Here we were lucky to get permission to park the caravan in a side street for a few hours. I did a quick change and then we drove down to the *South Wales Echo* where I was photographed and interviewed.

I had worked in these docks in the late 1950s as a foreman stevedore and a liaison superintendent for the Alfred Holt Shipping Company. I supervised their docking, discharging of Latex and their necessary sailing and docking arrangements.

From the *Echo* office we went out to a suburb called Clase to visit a good friend from those days. Dick and Lou Crees welcomed us with tea and cakes and we had a very enjoyable hour talking about times gone by. Dick had been particularly kind and helpful during a period when I was frequently ill and job security had been a worry.

We returned to the caravan to complete one more running session of about six miles to Pontlliw where we disconnected for the night. En route I ran very carefully through Morriston where I had spent five difficult and uncomfortable months in hospital.

At about 7 p.m. we were racing back to the Gower Peninsula to visit Dr Huw Griffiths who had looked after me so well when we had lived in Swansea. He was now retired and living in Langland Bay. We all sat out on the lawn drinking cool lagers with an incredible view out to sea and across the Bristol Channel to the northern coastlines of Devon and Somerset. We hope he enjoys his deserved retirement and envy him his uninterrupted view to Brazil!

We then dashed off further into the Gower Peninsula where my niece Kathy and her husband Martin had prepared a well-cooked and substantial supper. I still managed to fit in a hot bath but I wished I could have soaked for longer.

We were tired and it was after midnight before we got back to the caravan. After all the excitement and the rushing to and fro the daily total was still a very acceptable 35 miles.

Thursday 7 June was not a good running day. The legs just didn't want to work. I think both body and mind were close to going on strike. Instead of giving up we progressed in short and regular bursts—three or four miles at a time—and it adds up. It's no use pushing too hard and I think the body knows when it's being pressured. So, under these circumstances, I would walk rather than run. We were also held up for a short period with a slow puncture in one of the caravan wheels. Mr Rees of Cross Hands came to our rescue and kindly mended it free of charge. He also put a £1 note in our collection box.

It was a cool, overcast day as we by passed Carmarthen, ran through St Clears and finally parked a few miles east of Whitland. I was very tired after this shorter 30-mile day and was worried about a pain in my right leg. Friday 8 June I felt refreshed and there was no more pain in the leg. It was a lovely morning and the forecast was for fair weather in Wales. We breakfasted after passing through Whitland and entering the old county of Pembrokeshire. I now had to face a long and steep climb up to the small village of Llanddewi Velfrey — but what a wonderful view when I staggered to the top. It's what makes it all worthwhile. You do not have to be mad to be a runner but it does help!

To the north-west I had an excellent view of the Prescelli Mountains which would stay in view for the next couple of days as I rounded them from the south. It is from the slopes of Mynydd Prescelli that the great bluestones were hewn to build Stonehenge, the most famous of all prehistoric megalithic monuments. It has baffled scientists how these huge stones were transported from west Wales to Salisbury Plain but there's brawn and brains in Wales!

It was a much easier run into Haverfordwest along the A40. In fact, I ran through the town at about 1.30 p.m. and we parked just the other side for a late lunch. As I set off for St David's on the A487 Megan walked back into the town to do some shopping. It was now becoming really warm and I left my singlet in the caravan.

We had agreed to meet again by the sea at Newgale. I got there before Megan and waited impatiently for about half an hour. She arrived and, after parking the caravan, we thoroughly enjoyed an hour's relaxation on the beach while Merlin had her swim and expended a lot of energy chasing seagulls.

There was a very steep hill out of Newgale with a sharp left hand bend. The sort of hill you don't want to stop on when towing a caravan. Once again the scenery, either inland, towards the mountains, or out to sea across St Bride's Bay, was magnificent. It took away any tiredness and at times I felt I could go on running for hours.

It was 7 p.m., with yet another wonderful view, when I ran into St David's, with the sun setting over the western horizon. I didn't stop, but followed Megan through the town to a camping point two miles to the north, on the road to Fishguard. We disconnected and returned to the town to see the cathedral and eat out for a change. We felt that our arrival at the windy Land's End of Wales was some achievement and deserved a small celebration.

I had now been on the road for 21 days and completed 595 miles and today was my longest run — 38 miles. I admit I felt quite pleased with myself.

8

St David's to Chester through Central Wales

We thoroughly enjoyed the warm summer evening in Britain's smallest cathedral city, St David's. It's really no larger than a village. First of all, we spent nearly an hour looking round the very impressive cathedral which is situated in a sheltered hollow and less than a mile from the sea. It originated as a semi-monastic settlement founded by a sixth-century saint. It outlasted the Viking raids and was a flourishing community when the Normans came. William the Conqueror is known to have paid homage at the shrine of St David. The present building is constructed of grey and purple Cambrian sandstone hewn from local quarries and the work commenced soon after 1178.

We then strolled back into the village, where we found a delightful small restaurant, and settled down to a well earned evening meal. As a special treat the cathedral bell ringers were having a practice session. It wasn't until quite late in the evening that we finally drove back to the caravan. We hadn't been able to find a lay-by but I had managed to drive it up onto a very wide grass verge which was well clear of the roadside. The moon was shining, it was nearly 10.30 p.m., and yet I could hear a cuckoo calling somewhere far off in the valley. How quickly can the hustle and bustle of the industrial areas change to the peace and quiet of the countryside. At last I could feel reasonably satisfied with our achievement. We had now travelled over 500 miles in three weeks and almost everyday we were able to improve the daily average figure, which now stood at 28.33 miles per day. My left leg was a little painful where I had been hit by a chipping stone when a lorry passed me just after leaving Haverfordwest.

Another fairly early start, a cloudless day, and still the cuckoo is up before me! I have a small bruise from that chipping but it's not a problem. I suppose it's a risky type of accident that could happen when running on any newly tarred surface.

I was now looking forward to the journey through the Welsh countryside—most of which I would be familiar with from my childhood days and early youth. It was nice to be back with the hills, gorse and white-painted cottages.

It was a steady climb up to the village of Croesgoch where we stopped for breakfast, sitting out with our deckchairs admiring the sea view. I could have sat there all day but I had to press on as we had arranged to meet the local newspaper reporter in Fishguard at 11 a.m. With such a hilly course it was difficult to know how long it would take us. There was very little traffic and for company I had skylarks and sheep. The last couple of miles to Fishguard were very warm and the steep hills didn't help!

I reached the little square in the town and was surprised to see Megan waiting for me. She had already found a spot to park the caravan and it looked as though we would have to wait for the reporter. We got into conversation with a group of young men outside a pub and discovered that one of them, an ambulance driver, had seen me on a couple of occasions during the past week.

The young lady reporter arrived about ten minutes late and was determined to comment on my missing couple of front teeth. I had lost the plate sometime during our first or second day out from Wool.

We had lunch in Fishguard and then drove a couple of miles to Goodwick to look at a house belonging to my eldest sister. It was empty and she was trying to sell it but she was finding it difficult to keep an eye on her affairs from the top of Dartmoor.

I was back on the run out of Fishguard just before 2.30 p.m. It was still very hot and I discarded my singlet. It was a steepish climb for the first couple of miles and then levelled off through Dinas Cross and on to Newport.

We were now north of the Prescelli mountains and just a few miles south was the prehistoric burial chamber at Cerrig-y-Gof.

Soon after Newport we took a short cut on the B4582. It's arguable whether or not this was a short cut in time because it was impossible to do much running as it was such a steep climb. Nevertheless, I enjoyed every minute of this peaceful and breathtaking scenery. With the green, sloping mountains to the south and the brilliant blue waters of Cardigan Bay to the north, the only sounds were the occasional cry of a gull or the bleat of a sheep.

We had a late afternoon tea at a high point hamlet called Glanrhyd before starting the easier downhill jog back towards the market town of Cardigan, which I reached as the town clock was striking six. Poets of all periods have waxed lyrical over the beautiful river Teifi which flows into the sea at Cardigan. The salmon and sea trout that thrive in its tree shaded waters are fished from Coracles—small traditional craft that have continued to use the river while relative newcomers have been forced elsewhere by the silting of the town's port.

I crossed over the fine seventeenth-century, six-arched bridge that spans the Teifi, beneath the remains of a Norman castle, and continued out of Cardigan along the A487. Megan had gone ahead to look for a camping site which she found in a disused council chipping site just beyond Penparc. This was another uphill climb but I wasn't at all tired and completed this three-mile stretch before 6.30 p.m. We had a quick supper, changed and were about ready to set off back to Cardigan to visit friends when we noticed Merlin had rolled in some tar! We struggled with spirit, some special oil, scissors, soap and hot water, but it was very difficult to remove. Finally, after half an hour, we gave up and hoped she wouldn't jump onto the seats while we were away.

Madge and Meurig Davies lived on the outskirts of Cardigan in an elevated position overlooking the estuary. Even though we hadn't met for several years, they appreciated my odd request for an immediate hot bath before sitting down to an evening chat. I first met Madge over forty years ago. She was one of the attractive daughters of Mr and Mrs Williams who were farmers, and neighbours of my late uncle where I used to spend all my summer holidays—at a place called Wstrws at Capel Cynon about 12 miles from Cardigan. It was Madge who looked after this difficult, eccentric but wonderful old uncle when he was too old and infirm to look after himself. Naturally our evening was spent reminiscing about the old days, when the days seemed so long and the summers all sunshine and no rain! It's odd how one seems to forget the depressing aspects of youth.

It was late by the time we got back to the caravan and, fortunately, Merlin had kept her tar to herself. Not such a long run today, but I was quite happy with 33 miles to add to the total.

Sunday 10 June was another warm, sunny day and I managed to make a fairly early start. When we parked in lay-bys on the main route it was quite easy for me to set off without disturbing Megan, thus enabling her to have an extra hour's rest. It was different if we were parked down a side road or, on the now odd occasions, when it was necessary to be driven back to the previous night's stopping point. Today, however, Megan overtook me fairly soon as we had planned to stop for breakfast at a small village called Tan-y-Groes which was only three and a half miles ahead. It was a quick breakfast as I was keen to complete a greater mileage than I had done yesterday and I was diverting at this point to run past, and visit, that hamlet where I had spent all my summer holidays. Megan was going to continue on the main road and we agreed to meet at Synod Inn some four miles south of New Quay.

My route was twelve miles which, making allowances for visiting and talking, would probably take me about two and a half hours. I felt quite at home on the narrow roads, grass banks with their gorse and whitewashed cottages. Apart from the occasional milk lorry I hardly met any traffic at all as I jogged through the small villages of Glynarthen and Rhydlewis. After six miles I left the minor roads and joined the A486 at Ffostrasol and, 20 minutes later, I was running down the hill to the little hamlet of Capel Cynon. It didn't look as though it had changed at all during the past 20 or 30 years. It only consisted of a row of whitewashed, terraced cottages, a small church, chapel and little village school.

I was desperately thirsty and called at one of the cottages hoping to recognise someone. It didn't take long before a small crowd assembled when I told them who I was. My late uncle, although quite eccentric (he was known locally, and affectionately, as the Mad Major!) had been a very popular man, especially during the Second World War when he was a private in Dad's Army (Home Guard). So, naturally, they were interested in this nephew and the older people were thrilled to talk about earlier days.

My uncle had been a small man in stature, an outstanding athlete and scholar. His mile record at Llandovery College stood for many years. In the First World War he won the Military Cross and two bars and then joined a small British Army contingent that went to southern Russia to support the White Russians against the Bolsheviks. In July 1920 he returned to England and was discharged from the Army with a full disability pension.

For about 30 years he rented a large country property near Capel Cynon and had the shooting rights over about a thousand acres of heath land. My brothers and I were very fortunate to be able to spend all our summer, and often Easter and winter holidays, with this talented and remarkable man. He taught me so much about birds, their nests and their feeding habits. I can remember spending all day making climbing irons for me to investigate a hawk's nest—I was terrified!—and all one morning hiding in the heather watching a stonechat building its nest in the bottom of a gorse bush. I remember 'Richard' the buzzard that he left in the garage all one summer until it revived from an injured wing. For several succeeding years he used to regularly circle lazily over the house giving his plaintive 'peeiou' call before sailing off to quarter the heather moors in search of prey. As I grew older he taught me how to shoot grouse, blackcock, partridge, rabbits etc. It was wonderful to witness his well trained pointer dogs working the heather moors in pairs and suddenly freeze when they scented a covey of grouse. The best pair, who worked beautifully together, were Tandy and Shamus. In the spring he took me out fishing.

Eventually I went into Evan's little cottage, where it was cool, and enjoyed two glasses of orange squash. Evan was the son of Hannah who used to come and do some cleaning and washing for my uncle one or two mornings each week. I was very sorry to hear that Hannah had died, and so had her other son, Trevor. I remember her being so proud of Trevor, who became a fighter pilot, but in the early 1950s apparently his aircraft crashed and he was killed.

From Capel Cynon I climbed up the hill and at the top took the narrow lane to Wstrws Farm. My uncle's property had been adjacent to the farm and I knew it had fallen down but I didn't expect to find that it had totally disappeared. There was nothing left, no foundations even, and you wouldn't have known a house had ever been built there. I found it very sad that there was absolutely no evidence of this home where I had spent so many happy holidays.

I got back on the road again and almost immediately was passing another whitewashed and isolated cottage and I wondered what had happened to Joe Oil and Mary Pwth Gravel. I never knew Joe and Mary's surname but as Joe always drove an oil lorry he was known as Joe Oil for miles around and Mary was known by the name of the cottage, Pwlth Gravel!

Another quarter of a mile and I was at the top of the hill and it was here that I realised that the moorlands had also disappeared. From this vantage point, just after the war, heather moors were on either side of the road and covered about a thousand acres. Now it

7 Meeting our friends, Meurig and Madge Davies, at Synod Inn.

had all gone. There wasn't a twig of heather to be seen anywhere. I looked at the banks on the side of the road where hundreds of people used to stop and pick blueberries (we called them wortleberries) but these plants too had disappeared. A mile down in the valley I could see Ty'r Rhos, one of the moors that used to have marsh and bog land at its furthest extreme. It was here that we had once looked for the hen harrier, shot blackcock and, in the early autumn, we had picked the little red, buttonlike cranberries in the mossy bog. Here, instead of being replaced by green fields, was a forest of firs. The landscape as I had known it had completely changed and the house itself had disappeared. At this moment I wished I hadn't returned.

It took me another half an hour of easy running to reach Synod Inn where Megan was parked outside the pub. To our delight and surprise, ten minutes later Madge and Meurig turned up. They had decided on a Sunday morning drive and wondered whether or not they would meet us en route. I shall always be grateful to Madge and

Meurig for looking after and being so kind to my uncle in his twilight years. Next year, 1985, their son Hywel would win the Grand National on 'Last Suspect'.

I wanted to press on, so after a few photographs I set off towards Aberaeron where we planned to have lunch. This six-mile stretch I completed in just under the hour and Megan had fortunately found an excellent lay-by overlooking the sea, just south of the town.

Aberaeron's days as a busy seaport are long gone and today it performs useful services as an elegant and unspoilt holiday resort.

I was hoping to reach Aberystwyth as a minimum target for the day, after which Megan wished to visit her aunt, who lived an hour's drive inland. This would give me the opportunity for another soak in a hot bath. I had a couple of small blisters on my feet which I wanted to cure before they threatened to become a problem. So, after our lunch of salad and fruit and an hour's rest I set off northwards along the coastal road.

It wasn't the easiest route for running as we seemed to be meandering along the cliffs about 500 feet above sea level for a couple of miles and then suddenly it would be a steep downhill run into a small village, followed immediately by a steep climb up the other side. The rewards were the views across the sea into Cardigan Bay to the west and the mountains to the north and east. Mingled with the smell of the salt and the sea was that of the newly mown hay.

First came Aberarth and then Llanon, which seems to be a retirement place for old sea captains with shipshape cottages named after the craft they once commanded. Late into the afternoon I ran through the little village of Llanrhystyd with a stream bubbling down its main street and the beach just half a mile away.

I caught up with Megan just a short distance further on and stopped for a tea break. We were now about seven miles from our turn-off point into central Wales. Our course would not be taking us into the town of Aberystwyth, just to the outskirts.

From Llanrhystyd the road was a little more hilly until we reached Llanfarian where I crossed the river Ystwyth.

In the summer of 1938 my eldest brother, Robin, had decided to cycle from our home in mid Wales to my uncle's home at Capel Cynon in Cardiganshire. Although only ten at the time I had persuaded my parents to allow me to accompany him on this 72-mile journey over the Cambrian Mountains. It was somewhere near

Llanfarian that I fell off my bicycle and badly bruised one of my arms. If I remember correctly, it took us about eight hours to complete that journey and I don't suppose I would have ever dreamed that one day I would actually run over the same course many years later.

It was close to 6 p.m. when I crossed the river Rheidol at the approaches to Llanbadarn Fawr. I was sorry that we would not visit the university town of Aberystwyth. It's a friendly place, proud of its National Library of Wales, and a convenient tourist centre for exploring the Rheidol and Upper Wye Valleys. What makes the town interesting and exciting is the balance of the young and the old, the students and the retired, and the seat of learning for the young and the experience of the elderly. The setting, in the centre of Cardigan Bay, is idyllic with the mountains to the east, the sea to the west and a mild winter climate.

Megan was parked and waiting near the centre of Llanbadarn Fawr and, as soon as I jumped into the car, we drove off looking for a convenient parking point for the night. We didn't find one until we reached the village of Goginan on the A44 about six miles further on.

Our parking spot was opposite the local pub and, after a quick change, we set off at great speed and a long drive for supper with Megan's Aunt Enid at Caio. This journey took us back along the coast to Aberaeron and then inland to Lampeter and Pumsaint.

Megan's Aunt Enid is a very determined old lady and believes it was on her farm land of Maes Cadog that Caradog made his last stand against the Roman legions. He was captured and taken to Rome, where he was called Caractacus, and so impressed the Emperor Claudius that he was finally pardoned and freed. I sometimes think Aunt Enid would have been a match for any Roman warriors!

It was 11 p.m. when we left Caio and drove past the Roman gold mines at Pumsaint and it was nearly midnight when we reached Llanbadarn Fawr. I persuaded Megan to let me start running the six-mile leg back to the caravan while she went on and made up the beds etc. I didn't really enjoy running so late at night, even though it was quite light with a half moon, so I was quite pleased when Megan returned and picked me up about two miles short of my destination. Quite an eventful day and the first time I had run over 40 miles (41, to be exact).

Monday morning, and we both got up early as Megan had to drive me back down the road for a couple of miles to my near 1 a.m.

finishing point of the previous night. So I was back for breakfast within 20 minutes.

Fortunately, it was another lovely day as we attempted to cross the Cambrian Mountains into central Wales. From Goginan it was walking only and I progressed slowly up the mountainside, with its forestry plantations on either side, until I reached Ponterwyd where again I crossed the river Rheidol. Here we were four miles south of its source in the Nant-y-Moch Reservoir and three miles north of Devil's Bridge where this river narrows to form a spectacular 500 ft deep wooded gorge. Looking northward, and about 20 miles distant, I could see the mountain of Cader Idris. In 1945 I had set off from the Outward Bound Sea School at Aberdovey with an expedition party to climb this mountain. It was all part of the training course. Unfortunately, we didn't do very well and I remember being disappointed at our failure. It was one of those wet, drizzly and misty summer days and we got hopelessly lost and they nearly sent out the mountain rescue team to look for us. We should have managed because we had been properly trained for the event and equipped with compasses. However, it was all experience and great fun.

Today the weather was glorious and I could see up the coast almost as far as Harlech. I didn't bother to hurry as the climb was so steep and I was determined to enjoy this wonderful, peaceful scenery. Some bluebells were still surviving and I think it was a type of larch tree that had pretty little red cones. Regularly a cuckoo was calling from one valley and being answered in another and the only other sounds were the skylarks, sheep and an occasional vehicle.

As I strode on up towards the summit of Plynlimon I felt my feet were getting particularly hot and assumed they would soon cool down once I could start running again. It reminded me of the old drovers' road further to the south where the Welsh used to drive their cattle across these Cambrian Mountains to the English markets. At Tregaron, to prepare them for this long walk, the Welsh Black cattle were shod with metal shoes, the pigs with leather heeled socks and the geese were herded through a mixture of tar and sand. I think I would have joined the queue with the pigs—provided they didn't object.

At about 12.30 p.m. I caught up with Megan just beyond Eisteddfa Gurig where the road bears easterly and the summit of Plynlimon is a couple of miles to the north. This 2,470 ft mountain is the source of the mighty Severn, the lovely Wye and several lesser but equally vigorous rivers. From its summit the view encompasses virtually the whole of Wales from Snowdonia in the north to the Brecon Beacons and Black Mountains in the south.

We rested here for quite a while and had an early lunch. It was now possible to do a little running, which was a bit of a change, but it was still very hard work. A mile before reaching Pant Mawr we crossed over the early beginnings of the river Wye and then the road followed it for the next four miles into the small and beautiful village of Llangurig set in this river valley amid high mountain ranges and thickly wooded flanks. (I still remembered this little village from our cycling return journey in 1938. That had been another lovely summer's evening and we had knocked on a cottage door to ask for a glass of water. It's strange how one remembers such small and insignificant incidents.)

Here we joined the A470 and took the northerly fork to Llanidloes. It was now nearly 4 p.m., still very warm, and I was about to freewheel, running downhill for the next ten miles or so. That was great fun.

It seemed no time at all before I was running through the tree-lined streets of Llanidloes, past the old Market Hall—a beautiful timber-framed building—now a museum of farming and other local industries, and out into the country again heading for Newtown. After the long and tiring climb through the mountains I was delighted to be running free and could almost cross off a mile every eight minutes and was determined not to stop while I felt so fit and enthusiastic. In fact, I caught up with Megan at one point and told her I didn't wish to stop for at least another hour.

Perhaps my luck was suddenly running out because as I entered the little village of Llandinam I could feel a nasty pain in the back of my left leg above the knee and that very quickly slowed me down.

Apart from being a pretty Severn Valley village, Llandinam was the home of my first girlfriend. Unfortunately, I can not even remember her name but we met on a school outing to Aberystwyth to see Shakespeare's *Macbeth*. I cannot remember that either. I must have been about 12 years old!

Unfortunately, it was some time before I caught up with Megan again and by this time I was reduced to a limping half walk and half jog movement. I had planned to camp a few miles beyond Newtown so at this point we were still about nine miles short of the day's target. I had already arranged to meet my eldest brother outside

Chester's Crown Court at 5 p.m. on Wednesday—the day after tomorrow—so I couldn't afford to lose any mileage. I rested with both feet up for about half an hour and then tried rubbing in some Deep Heat. It was still quite painful as I set off again and I didn't even attempt to run. I settled down to a steady walk and hoped that I could cover nearly four miles an hour. During the first hour I made steady progress and passed the old Roman village of Caersws. By 7.30 p.m. I was at last approaching Newtown.

Once again I met Megan, had some hot soup, a short rest and another application of Deep Heat. Megan went ahead to look for a camp site beyond the town. After she left I found the going was harder. I was not only reduced to a walking pace but had developed a very painful limp. I could only hope that I would not do too much damage to my leg. I should have quit at the last stop. It was a blow to my pride that I found myself limping through the back streets of Newtown—my birthplace—in the quiet of the late evening. Perhaps in my dreams I had imagined myself sprinting down the main street in triumph. In reality, I don't suppose many people would have remembered me as I left the town when I was just 15. Anyway, I was due back in the morning for an interview with the local Press.

It was very nearly dark when I spotted Megan about half a mile away in a lay-by and it seemed a very long and painful ten minutes before I managed to hobble those last few hundred yards. It took us another 20 minutes, down one of the side roads, to find a suitable camping site and I got into bed as quickly as possible and felt very worried about the prospects of running tomorrow. I felt quite pleased that I had run, in one day, *almost* from the sea at Aberystwyth over the Cambrian Mountains to a point just beyond Newtown, registering a total of 40 miles.

Looking through my curtain as I lay in bed I could see the white may, or hawthorn, which was in full bloom, reflecting like snow in the moonlight. It was another lovely, peaceful summer night.

On Tuesday 12 June we were up early as I had decided to clock up a few miles before driving into Newtown for the Press interview. We disconnected and left the caravan in the field and, once we reached the main road, I left the car as gently as possible. I was still very stiff but delighted to walk. I was so depressed the previous night I wondered if it would be possible to even put my foot on the ground for the next few days.

It was my younger sister's birthday today and I reflected on the coincidence that she was born in a house called 'The Rock' less than a mile from our campsite and close to the banks of the Severn. I remember that day clearly, in 1936, as late in that afternoon there was a violent thunderstorm with flash flooding. Two houses at a small hamlet called Mochdre were nearly washed away and the swollen flood waters of the Severn carrying trees, cows and sheep, were almost up to our lawn. The Good Lord did not appear to be very pleased with the new arrival in our family!

Fortunately it was level ground so I walked and hopped for the next hour and a quarter and then decided we would return to the caravan for breakfast. That effort, I reckoned, had added three and a half miles.

Breakfast became a set pattern—which suited us fine. Half a grapefruit each, cornflakes and one or two slices of toast and marmalade. I then, usually, had tea but sometimes a glass of milk. I didn't at any stage adopt a particular diet and the only tablets I took were two Boots Multivitamins each morning.

After breakfast we drove into Newtown and met the local Press outside the half-timbered Bear Hotel. It was market day with stalls set up all along the main street and I was pleased to see the town appeared to be thriving but a little disappointed that I no longer knew anyone that I could call on and see. After a short interview we strolled around the streets replenishing our depleted stocks of groceries, vegetables and fruit, and the exercise seemed to be improving my leg.

We got back to the caravan at noon and I was pleased when we had hitched up and left to continue our northward journey. I was now running along the A483 and for the next 20 miles the Shropshire Union Canal would be following the road, first on one side and then the other. So, there were plenty of coots, grebes and ducks to keep me company.

I was pleased with my progress and we finally stopped for lunch opposite the drive to Powis Castle just on the outskirts of Welshpool. It was now 2 p.m. and I had covered the ten miles half walking and half running in under two hours. My leg seemed to be getting easier and not stiffer.

Powis Castle is the finest and best preserved medieval castle in Wales. The foundations were laid in the thirteenth century creating a home and a Border castle which has never been unoccupied. In 1952 the castle and park passed to the National Trust. One of its famous owners was Clive of India who filled the rooms with works of art and on one of the terraces placed cannons captured at the battle of Plassey in 1757.

Welshpool is another attractive Welsh Border market town and it was easy to maintain a fairly steady pace as the route continued through open and level countryside. It was cooler today and there was the occasional passing shower, which didn't bother me as I seemed to dry off fairly quickly without feeling chilled. I stopped several times for a ten-minute rest, a drink and gave my legs a rest.

By 5.30 we had covered another ten miles when we stopped for tea near Llanymynech. We didn't stay too long as I wanted to reach Gobowen before making camp. So, it was nearly 6.30 when we set off on the last stage, hoping to cover another nine miles. It was still quite cool and the pain and stiffness had now completely disappeared from my leg but I tried to maintain a steady and careful pace, stopping fairly regularly for a short rest or just slowing to a walk. At one point I had to stop and kill a baby rabbit. The poor little thing had been run over by a car and was struggling in the gutter with a broken back.

It was quiet when I ran through Oswestry and I was tiring as I approached Gobowen but I carried on through the town for another couple of miles before stopping for the night. There wasn't a suitable lay-by so we took a side road and eventually parked near the centre of the village of Weston Rhyn. Although only a 30-mile day, I felt quite satisfied and I was able to telephone my brother to confirm my arrival time outside Chester Castle at 5 p.m. the following day.

On Wednesday 13 June we set off at our usual time of about 7.30 and after steady progress on a cool, overcast day, we were passing about a mile west of Wrexham at 11 a.m. on the new dual carriageway by-pass. North of the town we left the dual carriageway and joined up with the A483 direct route to Chester but waited until we'd passed through Rossett before stopping for lunch. I now calculated that it was six miles to the centre of Chester and we decided that our best plan was to find a parking point about a mile short of the city near the inner circle complex. Megan was understandably terrified of driving the car and caravan through the narrow streets of Chester at peak rush hour.

I set off on this next five-mile stretch around 2.30 and almost immediately ran into unexpected injury problems. Without any warning I had shooting pains up and down my left shin bone. I guessed it was what they call shin splints. It was extremely painful to run and not a lot easier to walk but somehow I kept going until I caught up with Megan in a lay-by. I decided to take over the driving and see how close we could park to the nearest inner ring-road roundabout. If necessary, I could go round the roundabout and come back again. We were in luck as I found a farm turning about a hundred yards from the roundabout and took the turning without hesitation. The farmer agreed we could park there so we quickly disconnected, retraced our steps the mile to my last stopping point and then I limped back to the caravan. We hitched the caravan back on and Megan decided she'd wait there and I would ask my brother to drive out and pilot her back to their home in Kelsall after I had met him in Chester.

I had just over a mile to go before meeting my brother, the Press and probably other Crown Court officials. All that was quite enough of a worry without the embarrassment of a limp.

I was determined to arrive on the scene in style, so I took three aspirins and set off at a quick walking limp towards Chester Castle.

I arrived in sight of the building with ten minutes to spare and immediately sat hidden on the pavement with my back to the wall. I needed the next nine minutes to persuade myself of the necessity of jumping up at the stroke of 5, setting off at a forceful stride towards the castle entrance looking as strong as possible and not the slightest indication of a limp!

It must have been the castle clock that I heard starting to chime and, as I rose to my feet, I discovered that the pain had eased. Presumably the aspirins were having some effect. I took a deep breath and set off at eight minute mile pace. Within a short distance I could see my brother waiting near the entrance to the castle and the Crown Court. We hadn't seen each other for a couple of years and I think he was quite impressed with my speed of arrival and punctuality. How deceitful we can get.

I can't remember exactly whom I met apart from the Press but I was amused and embarrassed to find myself the centre of attraction, sitting in the Judge's Chambers in sweaty running kit and enjoying tea and biscuits.

Our mention in the *Chester Express* a few days later was predictable with the headline 'Judge meets brother on the run'!

Robin, my brother, then drove off to escort Megan to his home while I was preparing to run there through the narrow and complicated town centre following Judge David Hughes in his car. I lost my guide when I ran the wrong way down a one way system but soon afterwards I found I had cleared the city. Poor Judge David Hughes. I can not remember what happened to him. He must have thought, 'this brother on the run certainly knows how to give the judiciary the slip!' The aspirin effect wore off and I was in real trouble. That day ended with me sitting down on the pavement again waiting for help. The pain was too much. I just couldn't run another step and I hoped desperately that it wasn't going to be the end of this adventure. I had been running 26 days and had completed a distance of 765 miles.

9

Uphill to Glasgow and Scotland

It was nearly 9 before I woke up on Tuesday 14 June. The previous evening my brother had finally found me sitting on the pavement with my back against a wall feeling very sorry for myself. The pain in my left leg was telling me that I had shin splint problems with a vengeance!

I'd reached a point called Vicar's Cross along the Chester–Kelsall road and about four miles out of Chester. I was grateful to be driven back to his home in Kelsall and certainly enjoyed the sympathy and special treatment that was to follow. Nancy, my sister-in-law, is an excellent cook and had prepared a wonderful roast lamb supper which was a great treat after our soup and salad diet in the caravan. After supper I propped my leg on a chair and Nancy bandaged it with an ice pack while I reclined with a large brandy and ginger ale watching the others clear the table and wash up. Later in the evening, after a second brandy, I was ready for my hot bath followed by Ovaltine, hot water bottle and a luxurious double bed. No wonder I didn't wake up until 9!

Unfortunately, my leg was still quite painful but I was determined to see if I could make some progress. Leaving the caravan behind, Megan and I set off about noon, with a packed lunch and thermos, towards Vicar's Cross—my point of finishing the previous evening.

The moment I tried to run I realised it was hopeless and it seemed pointless to put undue strain on an already injured leg, so I settled for a very slow hobble stopping every 100 yards for a rest. I felt it was important to make an effort to add some mileage each and every day whatever the problem.

About every 20 minutes Megan would stop the car and rebandage the shin with fresh ice from the bucket we had brought with us. By 5 p.m. the ice had melted and I gave up the 'dot and carry' struggle and decided to settle for a day's total of seven miles. We marked our stopping point on the map which was at Helsby, about six miles east of Ellesmere Port, and set off back to Kelsall to enjoy yet another roast joint, brandy, hot bath and special nursing care for shin splints. I was unashamedly taking full advantage of my injury! It looked as though we would be spending a third night with my brother which was an enjoyable thought on the one hand but frustrating from the point of view of progressing with my run.

Friday morning we set off much earlier—just after 9.30—and I promised my sister-in-law that we would be back for supper no later than 7. It was actually 10 before I stepped out of the car at Helsby to start the day's run and straight away I found my leg was much better than I had expected. I set off very carefully by walking the first mile then gradually jogging for a few hundred yards, resting, walking, jogging etc.

As the day progressed I found I was running more that I was walking which was a tremendous boost to my morale. Forty-eight hours earlier I had thought that there was little prospect of continuing the venture. I had visualised the need for at least a week's rest for the injury to recover and I just couldn't financially afford to sit on my bottom twiddling my thumbs for that length of time. So I was feeling quite excited that, with care, we would not need to abandon the run after all and there would be no need to return home to Somerset.

From Helsby we were following the A56 to Warrington where we would need to pick our route carefully to take us northwards to Wigan. On the map this looked like one big built-up area with a nightmare of motorways, dual carriageways and a cobweb of other major roads criss-crossing one another. I was thankful Megan wasn't towing the caravan and could, therefore, keep in touch with me fairly easily.

Soon after noon I crossed over the Manchester Ship Canal and saw Megan parked a few hundred yards on the other side. When I was at sea I was fortunate in only once having to make the journey up to Manchester by ship. It was quite a performance taking a 10,000-ton ship up that canal. All the masts had to be lowered and I think we were at 'stations' for nearly 12 hours on a bitterly cold January day.

I stopped for a short rest, a drink from the thermos, planned our course through Warrington and agreed to meet at the first lay-by after crossing the intersection of the M62 motorway.

Megan went ahead of me into Warrington and that was the last I saw of her for nearly 2½ hours. When I reached the town centre I found the signs quite baffling and they didn't seem to compare with the scrappy piece of paper on which I had jotted down my directions. It wasn't very difficult for me to ask for directions from a pedestrian and I began to wonder how difficult Megan had found it with the pressure of lunchtime traffic. I was thankful she hadn't got the caravan.

Sometime after 1 p.m. I reached the roundabout intersecting with the M62 but continued north, as arranged, to the first lay-by. I wasn't too surprised to find Megan very conspicuous by her absence! I guessed she might be heading for either Liverpool or Manchester and decided I would return to the roundabout and wait.

Back at the roundabout I sat on the grass verge and waited for half an hour, by which time I got restless and worried and decided to look for a phone box and contact Nancy. On the other hand I was concerned that if I left my waiting point Megan would drive past the moment I left. That was a risk I would have to take.

Fortunately, I found a box just a hundred yards down one of the other adjoining roads. I phoned Nancy, told her where I was and said that I would wait there until Megan eventually found me.

We had previously agreed to phone Nancy if we should, for some reason, become separated and I had a tiny little pocket in my shorts in which I could carry a few coins for such emergencies.

It was nearly 3 p.m. before Megan finally arrived—I don't think she knew exactly where she'd been—and to confuse matters there was a misunderstanding as to our meeting point. However, we phoned Nancy again to say we had rendezvous'ed and were back on course. It was inevitable that we should lose each other on occasions in these circumstances and travelling such a vast distance. Our problem was to work out a sensible method of regaining contact when these mishaps did occur. We didn't have mobile phones in those days!

One blessing was the weather. After an overcast morning it turned out to be sunny in the afternoon so I didn't get chilled waiting around.

After a late lunch we decided to continue our northward journey. At this point my leg seemed remarkably sound and I had completed 15 miles. We felt a further five miles wouldn't overstrain it.

At 5 p.m. I entered Golborne and, just as I was leaving the town I caught up with Megan parked at a garage. This was to be our stopping point for the day and, after filling up with petrol, we turned south for our 25-mile return journey to Kelsall.

As soon as we got back to Kelsall we hitched on the caravan so that we would be ready for an early start the following morning — or as early a start after breakfast as was possible. My leg was almost back to normal but I decided to rest it as much as possible so, after supper, I just sat and watched television as the others went off to look at the garden. I had yet another hot bath and went to bed early.

We were very lucky to get under way the following morning at 9.30 after an excellent gammon and egg breakfast. It took us well over an hour to reach Golborne and it was just before 11 that I was back on the road pounding my way north towards Wigan.

As Wigan was about five miles north we decided that Megan should steam ahead and look for a parking spot for lunch about two miles the other side of the A5106 to Chorley. It was really almost one big built-up area as one town seemed to join with the next and the roads were fairly congested. Sometimes I had a pavement to run on and at other times I had to share it with intruding vehicles. Fortunately, today was Saturday so there were few lorries around.

Wigan was well signposted but it was a good three miles further on before I caught up with Megan and was surprised to find a few green fields around us. After taking my normal hour and a bit for lunch, I set off towards Chorley with the sun occasionally popping through a dark, cloudy sky. The traffic had eased considerably and, after leaving Chorley, I joined the A6 just beyond the village of Barton. In fact we were within half a mile of the M61, the main railway and the Leeds & Liverpool Canal. The M6 and A6 follow each other to Carlisle. It was a relief to be back in the countryside.

Sunday morning I set off at 7.30 and it was cold and wet. I was thankful to stop early for breakfast after just four miles. It rained most of the morning but there was hardly any traffic apart from some cycling event. Scores of competitors kept passing me — I assume they must have been travelling in a circle — and I felt quite sorry for them. They looked colder than me and were working ten times harder. However, I suppose like me they were enjoying themselves.

I took a short cut through Catteral on the B6430 rejoining the A6 at Garstang and we lunched a mile beyond Galgate. After lunch the sun came out and by 3 p.m. I was running through the city of Lancaster. As I started to clear the city and head for Bolton-le-Sands the shin splint pain started up again in my left leg. Unfortunately it was nearly another four miles before I caught up with Megan and by that time I was reduced to a limp and the leg was quite painful. While

Megan made the tea I tried massaging it with liquid paraffin and finally putting on Iodex followed by a crepe bandage.

After a two-hour rest I set off again walking and managed to keep this up for just over another hour. At this point I was limping so badly that several cars stopped to offer help or a lift. About three miles south of Milnthorpe I had to stop and we found an excellent parking site about half a mile down a side road.

The day's total was 27 miles. It was a peaceful spot until our little spaniel, Merlin, almost went crazy chasing the curlew and plover who were determined to tease her.

Once again our future didn't look too promising. Commonsense seemed to suggest that this recurring injury of mine wouldn't disappear until I gave it a good rest. Furthermore, we had no idea how best to treat such an injury but to continue running seemed out of the question. On the other hand I was not prepared to sit around in the caravan for several days doing nothing. After discussing it for nearly an hour, I decided not to run a single step the following day but would walk instead. Having come this far we were not going to give up too easily.

I was desperately worried so I telephoned Bruce Tulloh for advice. There were three choices:

1 The sensible course—complete rest for seven days.
2 Give up and go home.
3 Keep a packet of frozen peas wrapped around the injury (replacing it at reasonable intervals) and try jogging gently. You may run through the injury or you may make it worse.

We purchased a packet of peas, followed advice number 3, and within a couple of days were back to A1 certificate at Lloyds! I'm not sure which is the most embarrassing, a bag of peas strapped to one leg or a parrot on your shoulder!

After a restless night I was up fairly early and I still felt quite lame. It took me nearly an hour to walk to Milnthorpe and as soon as I got to the other side I saw the caravan and so I stopped for breakfast. After breakfast I kept up a reasonable pace as far as Kendal, where, after a few enquiries, I was able to purchase some fuses for the car lights.

We were now on the edge of the Lake District and also the western side of the Pennines. Ahead of us and upwards was Westmoreland, Shap and Penrith. So far so good, and I was pleasantly surprised at my progress. It might be slow but at least we were moving. Megan stopped fairly regularly and dressed the guilty shin. Unfortunately we hadn't got any ice so it was Iodex or nothing.

As we climbed higher and higher into the mountains and towards Shap the day got sunnier and warmer and the scenery was beautiful. I was amazed at the walled in fields. Hundreds of these dry stone walls all extending right up to the mountain tops and dividing the land into small fields of about four acres. I wondered how old the walls were and who had such patience to build them.

There were some beautiful views as I looked back down the valleys. This patchwork of dry stone walls, the sheep, the abundance of wild flowers and the songs of the skylarks and meadow pipits were such an enjoyable and peaceful environment. Perhaps the wild flowers survive so well because they don't use so much insecticide up here. For mile after mile there appeared to be a huge gas line laying project in progress. No doubt in due course the damage done to the countryside by these huge bulldozers would be repaired by the contractors. Some time later in the summer I recall reading somewhere that they unearthed a Viking or Roman canoe in this area.

It was 6 p.m. when we passed through the village of Shap and it had been a long, steady climb all the way from Kendal. I would have had to walk most of the way even if I had been fit.

We continued for another three miles before finding a suitable camping site. I was astonished that I had started the day limping, had been on my feet for nearly 12 hours, covered 30 miles and climbed over 1,000 feet and felt better now that when I had started. It just didn't seem possible — or even right that it should be so. Perhaps it was some special reward for perseverance.

We were up early on Tuesday the 19th and I was actually on the road by 6.30. Although my leg felt 100 per cent back to normal I decided I would walk for the first hour. Megan had set off looking for a lay-by about four miles ahead, which would give her plenty of time to sort out the caravan and prepare breakfast.

Through my niece in Newcastle we had contacted a dentist who had two practices, one in Hexham and another in Newcastle. On our first day out in May I had lost my dental plate with a front tooth and Megan was determined I should do something to improve my looks. So, an appointment had been arranged for me at 2 p.m. in his Hexham surgery and our plan was to run to the outskirts of Carlisle, dump the caravan in a lay-by and drive the 40 miles eastwards to the edge of the Pennines, to Hexham, have the necessary impression taken and the plate finally fitted when we reached Newcastle on our southward journey several weeks later.

We stopped for breakfast just beyond Clifton. I had no difficulty with my leg and had kept up a fairly brisk walk. It was a fine but coldish morning and we were now approaching the outskirts of Penrith. The A6, M6 and the main railway were all running close together. One moment both the M6 and the main railway were to the east but now they were both to the west and, at one point, a couple of miles back. I was in the centre.

We were situated between two mountain regions, the Lake District with the Cumbrian Mountains to the west—Ullswater was about five miles away—and the Pennines to the east.

After breakfast and an hour's break I set off at a steady jog. Although it was still hilly, on balance we were slowly losing height and the going was reasonably easy. Megan had gone ahead to look for a garage as the indicator lights were not working properly on the caravan. I met her again on the far side of Penrith where she told me there was a caravan centre which specialised in electrical problems about eight miles ahead near High Hesket.

Fortunately, it was on the main road so, after a hot Bovril, she left to get the problem sorted out and agreed to wait there until I arrived. It was nearly midday when I eventually reached Mason's Caravan Centre and spotted a couple of busy electricians trying to sort out what looked like miles of coloured cables in the boot of the car. It took them over an hour to finally resolve the problem. The owner was so sympathetic with our cause—and must have thought our need was greater than his—that he waived any charge for their services. I made a note to send him a postcard if we reached the point of 'mission accomplished'.

This delay put us a little behind schedule so, after running a few miles beyond Low Hesket, I caught up with Megan in a lay-by. While I disconnected the car, had a quick caravan wash and changed into normal clothing, Megan had filled a thermos and cut some sandwiches. Within ten minutes we had set off for Hexham about 42 miles away and we had just over an hour to reach it for my 2 p.m. appointment.

Since mid morning the clouds had cleared, it was a lovely sunny day and the scenery was magnificent. Megan drove while I relaxed and enjoyed both the views and the packed lunch. We reached Hexham with five minutes to spare and had little difficulty in finding Mr Davidson, the dentist, who performed his task fairly quickly.

Hexham is a delightful, bustling little town where we spent a good half hour replenishing our larder with groceries, followed by a rest on a park bench quenching our thirst with an ice cream. At this latitude the width of England, from east coast to west coast, is only 70 miles and Hexham is situated on the river Tyne, equidistant from either coast. It is surprising that to the north of St Bees Head on the west coast the widening plain of Cumberland has yielded only scattered and unimportant evidence of prehistoric settlement. There are no Iron Age forts, complexes of stone circles or megalithic burial chambers to indicate the presence of organised communities in the centuries before the Roman conquest. The role of the region in the human geography of the North West was profoundly changed in the early part of the second century AD. Under the orders of Emperor Hadrian the Romans built a wall 73 miles long, stretching right across northern England from Bowness-on-Solway in the west to Wallsend-on-Tyne in the east. (Or, for quick recognition on a map, Carlisle to Newcastle.) Its course was plotted from one natural vantage point to the next and it was built of the materials most readily to hand which were generally stone in the east and turf in the west. Along its length were twenty or so major forts and also a number of signal stations. It was built to discourage the Scottish tribes from marauding into the largely pacified territory to the south. The Roman occupation of the North West transformed the exposed lowlands in the region from a rejected and neglected area into an important zone of settlement.

On our way back from Hexham we decided to visit this famous structure as we'd spotted several signs to Hadrian's Wall on our incoming journey. We turned off the main road at Bardon Mill and after three or four miles of narrow roads we reached the viewing point. This section on the wall was built of square stones and the wall itself seemed about five feet high and about the same width. It was in an excellent state of repair and looked as though it was built about 20 years ago—not nearly 2,000! From this particularly beautiful elevated view point you could see the wall undulate across the rocky spine of Britain to the horizon. Here the wall reached its highest point of over 1,000 feet where it crossed the extreme northerly sections of the Pennines and the southern slopes of the Cheviot Hills. This major engineering achievement still stands as a remarkable monument to the

8 Megan and Merlin on Hadrian's Wall.

Roman occupation of Britain, still proclaiming the might of the Roman empire many centuries after its collapse.

After our dash to Hexham and a quick tour of Hadrian's Wall, we eventually returned to base soon after 4 p.m. and were delighted to see that no one had pinched our caravan. After hitching on and a quick cup of tea I was ready to set off to run through the city of Carlisle. I estimated it was about six miles to the city centre and a further three miles to the A74 dual carriageway which would take us almost all the way to Glasgow.

I'd arranged to meet Megan at the start of the dual carriageway. I thought she'd be able to find a lay-by close by or be able to pull well over on the hard shoulder. I'd had a good rest, so the run into Carlisle was quite relaxing and, although it should have been peak hour traffic, it didn't seem to be particularly busy. My route seemed to take me through mainly residential parts of the city with wide open pavements. At one point, obviously near the centre, I got a little lost with a complicated roundabout system.

The climb out of the town was quite steep but it was all quite easy going with parklands on my left and many young office people enjoying their summer evening stroll home.

Carolyn Etheridge's home was in Carlisle. She was my companion in the London Marathon, but she was away on holiday so unfortunately we would not be meeting each other on this occasion.

I reached the A74 about 5.45 p.m. and, although there seemed several opportune parking spots, there was no sign of Megan. Once again I was in a dilemma and didn't know quite what to do. I decided to wait a while near the roundabout. After half an hour I joined up with two young American girls, with huge packs on their backs, who were trying to hitch a lift. I explained my problem to them and asked them to persuade the driver of their lift to stop if they saw Megan parked by the roadside. The two young ladies were delighted to help and seemed fascinated by my story. I seemed to confirm their thoughts that most Brits seemed to be half off their tracks!

About five minutes after they left I spotted Megan, minus caravan, speeding southwards towards me. Apparently she'd been hooted off a parking spot by some big lorry and was forced to continue her journey up the A74. When she found a lay-by it took her nearly 20 minutes to disconnect and then she had to drive on another ten miles before reaching a roundabout to return in the other direction. No wonder she was late. It took me a further half hour to run to the caravan and then we drove it down a nearby side road where we found a quiet spot for the night. It wasn't a bad day's total of 34 miles.

The actual boundary separating England and Scotland runs from the mouth of Solway Firth in the west, just south of Gretna Green and about nine miles north of Carlisle, across the Cheviot Hills, and then follows the river Tweed through Coldstream to just north of Berwick on Tweed in the east.

Wednesday the 20th was another 6.30 start. It was a joy to hear the curlews busy in the fields and there was no shortage of rabbits. The ox eye daisy appeared to be the most popular wild flower in this area.

It seemed that I hadn't been running for more than about 20 minutes when I passed the turning to Gretna Green. I realised that we were now in Scotland although I hadn't noticed any sign to this effect.

It soon became apparent that this A74 dual carriageway was a very busy road and a very high percentage of the traffic was heavy lorries. The hard shoulder was very easy to run on but its width was only about 18 inches. There was very little character or interest in the actual route. It seemed a vast, never-ending road which became very boring. With the juggernauts zipping past my shoulder it was surprisingly important to concentrate as the effect of these huge vehicles rushing past at 70 mph could be quite alarming. I've never been in a wind tunnel, but possibly the experience is somewhat similar. I don't believe it was particularly dangerous but every now and again, when my mind was wandering on other subjects and I was not concentrating properly, the sudden rush or suction of air almost made me trip. A fall could easily twist an ankle or strain a muscle. On very rare occasions the drivers used to blow their horns as they passed and the effect of that unfortunate event was to make me jump like a shot rabbit—particularly if it occurred later in the day.

We had agreed to run through the small market town of Lockerbie, just off the main road, at noon, where a representative of the Macmillan Relief Fund was going to meet us.

It was at Lockerbie in 1593 that one of the last border family feuds ended in a fierce battle at which the Johnstones killed Lord Maxwell and slaughtered 700 of his followers.

Our timing was spot on but, although I ran up and down the centre of the town several times, I did not meet or see anyone from the charity. It didn't surprise me, but I was disappointed nevertheless. Instead, we had a half-hour break while I helped Megan with the shopping. She then rejoined the main road and we met up for lunch about three miles further north.

So far it had been a clear and sunny day but it became cooler during the afternoon. I was starting to enjoy the scenery again as I ran through Johnstonbridge spanning the river Annan and, climbing a little now, to Beattock where I arrived just after 6 p.m. We found a quiet pull in just off the main road about two miles further on. The day's total was 36 miles.

After supper we spent an hour planning how best to negotiate both runner, driver and caravan, safely through the city of Glasgow. Eventually we decided that the following day's run must take us to the end of the A74 and about six miles south of Hamilton, and 18 miles from Glasgow city centre.

On the second day of the run into Glasgow Megan would stay in contact as long as possible and then head for a caravan camping site at Alexandria at the southern end of Loch Lomond. After disconnecting the caravan she would then come back and look for me. I would carry sufficient money to stop in a café or pub for a pie and a pint. So, before going to bed, I dashed into the little town of Moffat and booked Megan into a place at Balloch which was the next village to Alexandria.

Thursday 21 June turned out to be wet and cold. A 6.30 start was now becoming a regular routine. I also generally walked during that pre-breakfast period as I felt it acted as a sensible warm-up session for the body and preparing it for a further 30 miles of mainly running for the rest of the day. Hopefully this routine, by trial and error, would prove to be a good insurance against any further injuries.

After breakfast there was little opportunity to run as it was a very steep, winding climb up into the Lowther Hills. I had my weatherproof clothing on but still felt cold as we headed into quite gusty and misty driving rain. I noticed a dipper, who seemed to be following me, in a nearby stream as he flew from rock to rock and appeared to be enjoying the wet weather. Each time he alighted on a rock he couldn't keep still and kept bobbing up and down with his white bib as though he was curtseying.

As the morning progressed the weather got worse but at least the climbing stopped and I was able to get back to running a little. Unless conditions improved it was going to be difficult to keep on target. Alternatively, I would have to extend my running time until we achieved an objective.

About mid morning the 18-inch hard shoulder had disappeared and was replaced by a faint dotted line with a 6-inch gap. So for the next 20 miles every time I heard a lorry approaching I had to run on the uneven grass verge. It was quite hazardous with broken bottles, tins, stones, bits of wire and hidden road drainage ditches. To these over-taking lorries I must have looked drunk as I dodged from one obstacle to the next one at the same time being buffeted by the very gusty and strong head winds. At times the driving rain felt like piercing needles.

We stopped for lunch soon after passing through Abington and I changed completely as I was both wet and very cold. Nevertheless, I was pleased that we had covered about 18 miles and it looked as though we were now on the other side of the Lowther Hills and the Southern Uplands and entering the plains of Lanarkshire. Unfortunately there was no sign of the weather abating and, a little later than intended, I restarted my afternoon session about 2.15. Megan set off at the same time intending to stop for petrol at the first service station.

After running for about ten minutes the main road divided with the A702 bearing right to Edinburgh and the A74 bearing left and uphill towards Glasgow. At the top of the hill was a service station where I found Megan had refuelled, and I stopped for about five minutes to help her fill our water containers which were running low. The woman petrol attendant looked puzzled on my arrival and asked me what I was doing running on the main road on such a wet, miserable day. My explanation brought a look of complete disbelief and there were no further questions.

One small consolation was that the wind had died down and the rain was more a light drizzle, but it was still very cold for late June. I felt I was running much more slowly than usual and walked for quite long periods which I think was due to the particularly cold weather rather than tiredness.

At tea break I changed all my clothing for the third time in an effort to feel warmer and more energetic. Megan was having difficulty in drying the garments with the car heater and washing anything was out of the question.

Finally, at a place called Blackwood, we came to the end of the A74, which we had followed all the way from Carlisle. At this point we were about 20 miles from the centre of Glasgow and the main approach road was taken over by the M74 motorway. As motorways were not permissible to runners we took the B7078 and Megan started looking for a suitable camping spot. About two miles further on we settled for a narrow plot just inside a farm lane turning.

After changing yet again, we returned to Blackwood to make several phone calls and bought fish and chips for our supper. I went to bed early and fell asleep quite quickly as I think I had used up more energy than normal in trying to keep warm and battling against strong head winds.

I was looking forward to reaching the city of Glasgow. It was our home port for Clan Line Steamers Ltd, and their ships were all built on the Clyde at Greenock. I would then feel I was really back in Scotland.

Not surprisingly, the weather was still wet and cold when I started my dawn run on Friday 22 June. We realised the roads would become particularly busy as we approached Glasgow so we decided to stay together as much as possible but knew it would become increasingly difficult for Megan to find convenient parking points.

We managed to pull in for breakfast at the entrance to some huge country estate near the centre of Larkhall but by 10.30, as I ran into Hamilton, I guessed we had lost each other. I assumed Megan would now make for the caravan site at Balloch and hopefully sort out about ten days' washing before returning in the afternoon to look for me equipped with thermos and sandwiches.

The run into Glasgow seemed endless and I thought the drizzle would never cease. I remember buying a Mars bar and eating it in a bus shelter but I didn't stay too long as I began to feel chilled. Towards noon I found myself running through some of the slum areas with their awful tenement housing. When I passed through the notorious Gorbals district, a taxi driver refused to give me directions. He just wound up his window and drove off. At my size and in running gear I couldn't have looked very offensive. Once again I was lost and appeared to be on the south side of the river instead of the north. I think it was eventually the George V Bridge where I crossed over to the northern bank of the river Clyde.

As I joined the A814 to Dunbarton I passed under a section of another bridge and it was here that I saw several men sitting with newspapers covering their legs and, as I ran by, a small terrier dog rushed out from under one of the newspaper blankets and gave me a sharp nip just above the knee. I didn't stop to argue with the dog or with its master who I assumed was probably an alcoholic meths drinker. In fact, within a couple of hundred yards, I decided I too would stop for a pie and a pint. I felt I had something to celebrate as I was now in the centre of Scotland's largest city. It was exactly 35 days to the hour since I had left Wool in Dorset and I had covered exactly 1,000 miles.

The pub I picked was in a pretty rough area and was surprisingly busy for a weekday but I felt happy and relaxed in this friendly atmosphere. It's not everyday that we can quietly drink to the completion of a 1,000-mile foot journey. Nevertheless, although I was naturally delighted with the distance covered I was disappointed by the time taken. I didn't consider that an average of 28½ miles per day was particularly commendable. I would be looking for a considerable improvement in the time taken factor for the second 1,000 miles.

10

The Road to the Isles

After a pie and a pint (or rather, half pint) I was ready to tackle the run out from the centre of Glasgow towards Dumbarton. I emerged from the little pub at about 2 p.m. and set off at a gentle jog through crowded streets. There was an improvement in the weather as the rain had stopped, but it was still overcast. I was now heading downstream towards Partick and Clydebank but at this stage I didn't have a view of the river itself. I was still in a very poor area with streets and pavements strewn with litter on both sides of the road which were overlooked by large tenement buildings. Most seemed badly in need of repair and it was depressing to realise that they still housed young working couples with children or the elderly. They couldn't possibly be suitable homes for either. As I approached Clydebank I noticed that a number of these buildings were being demolished. Not before time. I could remember them when I first came to Glasgow in 1946.

After a couple of miles the road widened and I found it easier to run down the narrow strip on the central reservation than on the crowded pavements, provided I was careful to look both ways at each intersection before crossing over.

I knew I had about ten miles to run from the pub before I would be free of the city but, just before this happened, I suddenly found that the route divided into a dual carriageway system and for the first time there was no hard shoulder and no pavement. It was quite a frightening experience as there was just a wall, then the road and a metal barrier between the two carriageways. Probably I wasn't supposed to be running there but it was too late to make any enquiries. I felt vulnerable and boxed in, with the one-way only traffic travelling at high speeds, but fortunately it only lasted for a couple of miles.

Suddenly the slums and the city streets had given way to more open country, with modern housing estates, and the sun was actually making an appearance.

At about 3.30 I ran under the new Erskine Bridge, which spans the river Clyde and joins the motorway to the north bank routes. I was now in an almost totally different environment. The sun was shining, the birds singing and it was virtually all countryside. The road now climbed up to a point called Bowling and from here I had my first good view of the river Clyde. Below me I could see the small Bowling Lighthouse which used to be our main marker when coming up river to berth in the King George V Docks. Downstream I could see Greenock on the south bank where all the Clan Line ships had been built.

There must be a lot of unemployment in that area and it's sad to realise that so many of the world's finest ships, like the pre-war liners *Queen Mary* and *Queen Elizabeth*, were built and launched on the Clyde. The majority of these yards are now idle with no prospect of any further ship building orders and the young men, with their skills, no longer required, utilise their time in the clubs, pubs or dole queues.

It was soon after passing Bowling that I spotted Megan driving towards me and I thought for a moment that she hadn't seen me and would speed on to Glasgow. Anyway, she turned round at the nearest road junction, overtook me and parked in the next bus stop. She'd brought a thermos, sandwiches, cake and a change of running shoes. It was an ideal meeting point as I was beginning to tire and I was also very thirsty. I never seemed to get particularly hungry but often thirsty.

Megan described in detail the directions for me to find the caravan camping site which I hoped to reach by 6 p.m. It was 5 when Megan left me and set off back to the caravan to cook supper. I estimated the distance to run at about seven miles.

It was another lovely evening as I set off on this last session for the day. All went well for the first couple of miles, until I reached the other side of Dumbarton, and then I ran into a very strong head wind. Although it remained sunny, this strong, warm wind persisted. At times it was nearly gale force and therefore too difficult to run, so I had to slow down to a walk. I always find a head wind more tiring than a steep hill and I was delighted to stagger into the campsite at Balloch, even though I was well over half an hour late.

I had no choice, I needed a shower but I don't like these lukewarm affairs. I'm not one of those tough people who enjoy cold baths and midnight swims. I'm soft. I like warm water, warm clothing and a warm bed.

The day's total was 36 miles so, after an excellent supper and an hour's TV viewing in the camp lounge, I went to bed. I didn't need rocking to sleep.

It was a cloudy morning and a little after 6.30 when we drove quietly out of the caravan camping site at Balloch. As I started my run from the nearby roundabout on the A82 I realised that we were entering a substantially different phase of our journey. It was difficult to appreciate that I would be running on normal country roads for nearly 700 miles, passing through only minor towns and villages, as we negotiated the northern extremities of Scotland and down its east coast to the city of Edinburgh. The only other major city would be Perth. Trunk roads and dual carriageways were going to be out of fashion for the next three weeks. The pace and volume of traffic would be much less but I had noted some very mountainous and worrying routes for caravan drivers, particularly a section in the extreme north-westerly corner of Scotland. So far Megan had coped very well and I could only hope that her nerves would remain intact. After all, she would soon be up to a rally driver's standard by the time she climbed the Highland roads! In so many ways Scotland was going to be quite a different chapter of our story.

It was now midsummer, the sun had reached the Tropic of Cancer and had just started its southerly journey. However, as we continued in the opposite direction, the hours of daylight still lengthened and by the time we reached Durness we were close to 60 degrees north latitude, less than 400 miles from the Arctic Circle where the sun doesn't set in summer.

Two miles after starting my run the road ran close to the shore of Loch Lomond and a few miles further on I stopped for a short break when I caught up with Megan and the caravan. She was strolling with the dog near the water's edge where there was a very large country mansion with a rhododendron hedge. Here we witnessed an interesting and amusing game between Merlin and a pair of willow warblers or chiff chaffs. (It's almost impossible to tell the difference.) We noticed her chasing one of these little birds for about 30 yards along the hedgerow when suddenly its partner swooped down, flying in the opposite direction, encouraging Merlin hastily to change course 180 degrees and give chase in the opposite direction. After a short distance the first bird took over forcing the dog to perform another acrobatic 180-degree turn. This unusual exercise repeated itself four or five times before the birds finally took their leave. We certainly got the impression that the birds were not necessarily protecting a nest, since they didn't seem angry or agitated, and so we assumed they were enjoying an early morning dog training session!

We stopped for breakfast at a place near Rossdhu House with a lovely view across the loch in one direction and the mountains rising steeply in the other direction. Unfortunately, just after breakfast, we were enveloped in that cold, misty drizzle which seems to be a popular part of Scotland's weather programme. I was quite warm in my Nike weatherproof running gear and fascinated by the loch's scenery. The road follows the loch's shoreline for its full length of 24 miles. Loch Lomond is the largest expanse of fresh water in Britain and is sheltered by wooded mountains that climb dramatically from its northern shores. One of these is Ben Lomond, rising to 3,192 feet, which we passed west of at about noon as we ran through the village of Tarbet where the loch narrows to about three-quarters of a mile across.

I kept running through the light shower for a further seven miles before stopping for lunch near the northern end of the loch, immediately under the shadow of Ben Vorlich which towered above us to a height in excess of 3,000 feet.

Our nervous and shy little spaniel seemed to have taken on some extra rations of courage. Before we started this journey she was terrified of water but, after lunch, she decided to chase some birds across the loch. After swimming for about 100 yards we were relieved when she decided to return to our shore and not to attempt the crossing!

As the evening approached the drizzle abated, and by 6 p.m. the sun appeared and the storm clouds disappeared. The running had been comparatively easy, with hardly any hills, so I kept going through Crianlarich and finally camped for the night just south of Tyndrum at a farm called Dalrigh.

While we were eating our supper the westerly sun was gradually setting behind Ben Lui and we could see a thin line of snow glinting in the sunlight near its summit and some clouds were beginning to roll over the mountain's peak.

We were discovering several varieties of bird life which were new to us. During the day we had seen several common sandpipers on the shores of Loch Lomond and Merlin had given chase to a greenshank during her last outing before bedtime. I think that was the only greenshank we saw, but later on the redshanks and sandpipers were constant companions.

Without much difficulty I was now running about 35 miles a day. The routine appeared to have settled down to starting at 6.30 a.m. and stopping at about 6.30 p.m., making it a 12-hour session. I seemed to have got over my injury problems and I felt that 35 miles running, spread over 12 hours, was an easy, sensible and safe daily pro-gramme. With so much daylight I might soon consider increasing the mileage but at the same time also increase the running time. In that way it shouldn't introduce any extra strain to the body. At the moment I was running about ten miles by 10 a.m., 20 miles by lunch at 1 p.m. and 35 by supper at 6.30.

Sunday 24 June dawned overcast but without any rain. I lay awake for quite some time before getting up, having my glass of milk and cornflakes and setting off at 6.30. Within half an hour I'd run through Tyndrum and reached Clifton where the road divided—left on the A85 for Oban and right continuing on the A82 for Fort William. Here the road also began to climb quite steeply into the Scottish Highlands and I struggled onwards and upwards for another couple of miles before stopping for breakfast.

The common sandpiper was becoming a regular and friendly sight on the edge of the roadside. It comes to Britain in the summer to nest beside the brooks, trout streams and lochs of the northern part of the kingdom. They have a shrill and distinctive song, given from the air, and they fly in a peculiar half circle low over the ground or water alternately flickering their wings and momentarily gliding. They are about the size of a blackbird.

After breakfast the sun came out, although it wasn't really very warm, but the countryside was wild and beautiful with just a sprink-ling of holiday traffic which included the occasional touring bus. About mid morning I found myself enjoying a slight downhill stretch and about a mile ahead I could see the car and caravan parked alongside a small loch. This was Loch Tullah which was a couple of miles beyond the Bridge of Orchy. The road was quite narrow here with no proper pull in and Megan got tooted a couple of times for holding up the traffic. I stopped for a drink and we also let Merlin have a run by the loch. Unfortunately there were quite a number of ring plover which swooped and teased the dog. This energetic little animal—which was becoming much fitter than me and ten times more excitable—nearly wore her pads off as she gave chase, first in one direction and then the next. She is so disobedient when hunting that we would have had as much success in calling the plover to heel as call her. Sadly, Merlin was beginning to develop Walter Mitty-type illusions that not only could she swim lochs but could almost fly. At least none of those birds were nesting so she really wasn't doing any harm by giving chase. It was just a matter of lack of discipline and upbringing from our point of view.

Later in the day we noticed that she was limping and, as we could find no evidence of cuts or thorns, we concluded it must be a muscle injury. Perhaps she too had developed shin splints.

From Loch Tullah the road began to climb again and when I noticed a big 'S' bend up in the mountains I decided to take a short cut through a very steep gully with rushes and coarse, tufted grass. By the time I emerged back on the road I'm certain I would have spent less time and less energy if I had stuck to the main route. Nevertheless, I enjoyed the change of scenery and it was good to get away from the tarred roads. The only danger was twisting an ankle in a rabbit hole.

After leaving Tyndrum I discovered that there were milestones every mile marking the distance back to Tyndrum in exact miles and the distance on to Kinloch in miles and quarter miles. I started to guess how long I would take between each stone and it's surprising how accurate I was—rarely more that 15 seconds out either way. When I was more than 15 seconds out I reckoned someone must have moved the stone. It was an amusing game to play to while away the time.

These were the Grampian Mountains and I was currently running on the high plateau of the vast, wild and desolate flat land of Rannochmoor with its open countryside. After passing close to another small loch called Bà we realised we were near to the approaches of Glencoe.

We stopped for lunch not far from the Kingshouse Hotel (where there has been an inn for centuries) and opposite the ski-lift to Meall a'Bhùiridh which rises to 3,636 feet. During lunch dark clouds began to appear and by 2 o'clock it had started to rain. There didn't seem any point in delaying my run as the wet weather looked set for several hours, so I donned my leggings and windproof jacket and set off into the eastern entrance to Glencoe.

The Massacre of Glencoe must surely be one of the most cowardly, brutal and treacherous acts committed by our troops against our own, mainly civilian, population. The troops had been billeted for nearly a fortnight with the MacDonalds of this glen and accepted and enjoyed the hospitality of these highland people when suddenly, at 5 a.m. on 13 February 1692, they set about murdering them in cold blood. Major Robert Duncanson had received his orders the previous day and the first sentence was very specific in its requirements: 'You are hereby ordered to fall upon the rebels, the MacDonalds of Glencoe, and put all to the sword under seventy'.

This narrow, rocky pass is about six miles in length under high mountains—great rocky peaks split by ravines on one side, soaring steep slopes on the other—above a flat, grassy floor, past a little loch and to the shores of Loch Leven. The MacDonald community was hemmed in by these towering mountains to the north and south so the trap was set by sending Robert Campbell of Glenlyon to seal the escape routes on the southern flanks, Major Duncarson with 300 soldiers stationed themselves at Invercoe to stop escapes at the mouth of the glen via Loch Leven and a final 400 troops were to march from Fort William through a gap in the mountains called the Devil's Staircase in a pincer movement to cut off escape on the eastern side of the glen.

After running for four miles the road began to narrow and I was starting to descend. Immediately on my left was the high mountain of Buachaille Etive Mór which stood like a sentinel guarding the approaches to the glen. This was also Altnafeadh where the troops from Fort William emerged in 1692 to seal this eastern trap. Fortunately they had encountered a severe blizzard in the Devil's Staircase and had arrived late. They only found one old man of 80 and promptly killed him.

It was quite an awesome feeling, running slightly downhill into this valley, steeped in history, with dark, low clouds and their mist and drizzle seemingly rolling towards me. The further I ran into the glen the more I was fascinated by these huge, rocky mountains towering over me and one could almost sense how easily one could feel trapped in such an environment. It was now a summer afternoon but the light was shut out by the low clouds and high mountains. I don't know how high the peaks were above the road running through this gorge, but the distance between some of the peaks, which were over 3,000 feet above sea level, was less than two miles across the glen.

Not only was I wet and cold, but there was a very strong wind blowing up the valley from Loch Leven. I was trying to enjoy and take an interest in my surroundings but the road was very narrow and it was difficult to take it all in. I always kept one eye on my footsteps, one on the on-coming traffic and occasionally borrowed one to look at the scenery.

About half way through the glen there was a parking space where I caught up with Megan who had prepared a hot Bovril and biscuits. I was short of dry clothing so I didn't stay long as I had decided I would end the day's run before changing my wet clothes. Luckily, as we reached the mouth of the glen, it began to open out into fertile green pasture lands. I hadn't enjoyed Glencoe. It felt an oppressive and depressing place. Even the scenery seemed grim and sombre but no doubt everything was much more cheerful on a warm, sunny day.

It was a relief to reach the edge of Loch Leven, where the rain had ceased, and I looked back at the dark mountains of Glencoe, still shrouded in mist and cloud. Later, in the winter months, a team of British mountaineers were to train in Glencoe for their attempt on the north face of Everest in 1985.

The total number of men, women and children murdered in the glen was 38, which was less than a tenth of those they had been ordered to kill. It is thought that many of the troops, sickened by the slaughter, had assisted in the escape of many of the MacDonalds. However, apart from the 38 killed, many others died as they struggled through the mountain routes in the arctic conditions of 13–14 February 1692.

Four miles further on a bridge took us across the mouth of Loch Leven and we found a camping site within half an hour near the shore of Loch Linnhe, just beyond Onich. Once again I had managed to cover 36 miles in those wet and mountainous conditions.

Monday 25 June was a lovely, sunny day which made life much more cheerful. I was trotting along the road at the usual time and, after a brief stop for breakfast, we reached Fort William at 10 a.m. This town is a major resort and touring centre for the Western Highlands situated near the west end of Glen Nevis and the head of Loch Linnhe. Fort William lies under Britain's highest mountain, Ben Nevis, which is another attraction for the tourist.

We stayed here longer than intended but it was a treat to be back in civilisation for a couple of hours. We called at the post office to collect our mail and replenished our food stores. After window shopping and an ice cream we were back on course at 11.30. Although Ben Nevis is over 4,000 feet it didn't appear to dominate its surroundings in the same way as the mountains of Glencoe did. 'The Ben' is more the gentle giant overlooking Glen Nevis—one of the most beautiful valleys in Scotland. Ahead of me was a ten-mile easy stretch to Spean Bridge, which I reached just before 3 p.m. In between we had stopped for lunch, sitting outside in our deck chairs enjoying the scenery. It was a cloudless and hot afternoon when I found myself running down into Spean Bridge where the caravan was parked opposite a large 'local industry' shop. I guessed Megan would be somewhere inside so I helped myself to a glass of lemonade before joining her in the gift shop. It was a quality shop with some very attractive woollen garments, not the usual holiday junk. A stranger suddenly tapped me on the shoulder and asked me where I was going and where I had come from. I was dressed in my running shorts with the Cancer Relief Fund singlet and it transpired that my stranger was a bus driver for a large bus company from Wigan. He did weekly bus trips to Scotland and he reckoned he'd seen me running on the road a couple of times during the last few weeks between Spean Bridge and Wigan.

From Spean Bridge the road began to climb steeply again and I was delighted to spot a colony of sand martins busily engaged feeding their young in a high sandy bank in what looked like a disused quarry. I hadn't seen these little birds for many years. Within a couple of miles the road levelled off and suddenly, on the side of the road I stopped to view the Commando Memorial, erected in 1952 by local subscription. This very striking and impressive memorial by Scott Sutherland was erected to the Commandos of the Second World War, many of whom, of all nationalities, trained in this area. The views from here to Ben Nevis are magnificent and near the memorial a minor road drops down down to Gairlochy where the Caledonian Canal climbs up two locks to Loch Lochy.

Soon the road passed through Invergloy where rhododendrons appeared to be growing wild over the immediate countryside and the views of Loch Lochy were quite spectacular. There was a temptation to keep stopping just to stand and admire this beautiful countryside of Scotland.

Late in the evening we passed the northern end of Loch Lochy, crossed over the loch gates which join it to Loch Oich and found a pull in just before Invergarry. It wasn't the best camping site as

Megan had got one wheel of the caravan stuck in a ditch and the local mosquitos objected to our presence. With a little perseverance and patience we overcame both problems.

Today's run was a mile down on yesterday's but quite acceptable. Perhaps tomorrow I would try to pay more attention to running and less to the scenery.

It was a clear but cold morning as I set off through Invergarry taking the left fork on the A87 when I reached the T-junction at the far end of the village, which was the route to Kyle of Lochalsh. The right fork was the continuation of the A82 to Inverness. The roads were so quiet and deserted of traffic that we allowed Merlin to run with me. Unfortunately she was so full of spirits and excitement that the moment she spotted a sandpiper she was off like a bullet. One moment she was lost and then suddenly she'd emerge, leaping out of the forest, dart across the road and, with engines at full thrust, give chase to the nearest wild duck or sandpiper at the edge of the loch.

Another new bird to us was the very attractive oystercatcher and this wader, with its bold black and white plumage and long orange bill, would be company for us all the way through Scotland.

When Merlin was in the car she would literally shiver with anticipation and excitement as she watched the bird life near the roadside. She seemed to be winding herself up ready for starter's orders.

It was mainly uphill from Invergarry and I was interested to spot a private graveyard by the side of the road with a circular wall and no apparent gate.

We stopped for breakfast overlooking Loch Garry on the one side and forest land on the other. It was here that we spotted our first siskin, a small yellow greenfinch once much admired as a cage bird under the name of Aberdevine. We didn't see many of these little birds but apparently this species is increasing because of the advance of the conifer plantations.

During the morning there was one downhill spell to Ceannacroc Lodge where the road turned abruptly from a northerly direction to a westerly. Not only was it an uphill struggle but I had to battle against a strong but warm head wind. This head wind continued for well over an hour as I ran and walked overlooking Loch Cluanie. I never realised that there were so many lochs in Scotland. Once again we were enjoying some quite spectacular views. About 4 p.m. the climbing stopped, the weather changed to mist and drizzle and suddenly it was all downhill. This was another narrow gorge called Glen

Shiel, not unlike Glencoe, with mountains towering over both sides of the glen and reaching heights of well over 3,000 feet. And the weather too had changed into low clouds with mist and drizzle. I kept looking up into the menacing peaks hoping a rock wouldn't slide off the top. After a fine, sunny day this last hour and a half was miserable for running. Even the downhill section was a strain as it was too steep.

It was pouring with rain as I passed over the river Shiel at Shiel Bridge but I continued for only another mile until giving up at a parking spot near the shores of Loch Duich. Visibility was down to about 200 yards with low clouds enveloping the mountains and hanging over the loch.

I changed quickly into warm clothes, disconnected the caravan, and we drove into the little port of Kyle of Lochalsh about 14 miles away. Here was the end of the road to the Isle of Skye and we hoped, on this summer's evening, that we would enjoy the famous and beautiful views across the sound to the jagged Cuillin Hills of Skye. As it turned out, the weather was so appalling that we could hardly see the end of our bonnet as we drove back to the caravan clutching our packets of fish and chips.

Wednesday 27 June I started a little earlier, at 6.15, and after crossing over the southern point of Loch Duich by bridge the road soon began to climb once again but it was the wet, miserable weather that was depressing me. It was difficult to keep dry and warm. The locals kept telling us what lovely weather they had had in May and seemed satisfied that they couldn't expect any more.

We stopped for breakfast just opposite Eilean Donan Castle which had been a base for a Jacobite Rising in 1719. It was partly destroyed by a British frigate during the ensuing battle, this particular rising being finally routed in Glen Shiel. The castle was left in ruins for nearly 200 years until restoration started in 1912 and took twenty years to complete. Eilean Donan was originally built in about 1230 to guard against Norse invaders.

I was still wet and cold as I set off after breakfast and after a mile I crossed over a bridge spanning the mouth of Loch Long. Although the weather didn't improve my body temperature began to rise as I pounded out the last couple of miles of our particular 'Road to the Isles'. This point was at Auchtertyre, a hamlet six miles from Kyle of Lochalsh. It was here that we were to branch north on the A890 and head further into the Highlands and remoter parts of Scotland. I paused for a moment, looking west along the A87 towards Kyle of Lochalsh and the Isle of Skye before turning right and heading back into the rain and the mountains. It was difficult to appreciate that I would have to run another 300 miles before I reached John O'Groats.

11

North West Highlands to Durness and John O'Groats

Climbing steeply north from Auchtertyre the rain began to ease and, as I glanced westwards, the Cuillin Hills of Skye were occasionally visible through the typical mists of Scotland. These peaks, reaching heights of over 3,000 feet, still dominated the seaward horizon and, through shafts of sunlight, the pastel green colours appeared to merge into the horizon.

It was almost impossible to run in these wet and hilly conditions and it took me nearly two hours to cover the next six miles to a position high above the village of Stromeferry where I found Megan parked and anxious for me to disconnect the caravan so that she could drive down to the village for groceries. During her absence I helped myself to several cups of hot Bovril and changed my soaking socks and shoes. I noticed that, for the first time, I was developing blisters on the underside of my big toes. I suspect I was not changing my socks or washing my feet often enough but washing and drying were becoming quite a problem.

It wasn't until late in the afternoon, alongside Loch Dughail, that the rain finally abated. It was here that we stopped for tea and I prepared myself for the final evening session. I was so often surprised that I ran better and further in the evenings than at any other time and it seemed like getting a second wind. Today was no exception and, with the change in the weather, I was able to enjoy the soft green forestlands of Glen Carron. Wild irises, raspberries, roses and rhodo-dendrons are quite common in the Highlands.

I kept going until nearly 7.30 p.m. when Megan had found a spot just wide enough to back the caravan clear of the road. We were opposite a small loch called Sgamhain where I could see a lone fisherman optimistically casting his line into the shallows. While

Megan was cooking supper I set off up the side of a steep hill that was overlooking us as I had spotted a red deer looking down from a rocky crag as I was manoeuvring the caravan into its parking position. When I reached the crag there was, of course, no sign of the deer but I had a wonderful view for many miles in most directions. Through the binoculars I was lucky enough to witness the rightfully optimistic fisherman landing a trout which looked a fair size. I didn't stay too long as I was beginning to tire and I felt that mountaineering was an unnecessary extra exercise. I was surprised that the day's total was our equal best of 38 miles.

Although we were thoroughly enjoying this period in Scotland, the constant wet and drizzly weather was a great disappointment. It had an adverse effect on morale and meant that providing dry clothing was a constant problem. I therefore decided that we should attempt to increase our daily mileage a little so that we could escape sooner from this wetter part of Scotland.

So, Thursday 28 June saw me on the road well before 6.30 and after half an hour I caught up with Megan who was very excited about a couple of deer that she had seen. As the road was deserted of traffic Merlin joined me for the next few miles and we left Megan scanning the horizon with binoculars looking for more deer. Almost immediately we reached the tiny village of Achnasheen with its railway halt, hotel and a few cottages. Here I joined the A832 at the head of Bran Valley and I was pleased that Megan overtook me and indicated that she would stop for breakfast at the first opportunity as a dark and threatening cloud was rolling up the valley. As I felt the first drops of rain I managed to sprint to the caravan and shelter before the heavens opened.

By 10 a.m. the rain had stopped and the sun was shining so I set off down this long valley. It looked like being a 'bird' and 'river' day. Oystercatchers and sandpipers followed me for most of the day and during the morning I picked up a meadow pipit that had only just died. Its little body was still warm. The valley was criss-crossed with small streams and large rivers and I saw several dippers bobbing up and down on the mid-stream boulders. At one point during the day I almost stepped on a redshank. He was so tame, or perhaps frightened, that at first I thought he was injured.

As I reached Loch Luichart the peace and quiet of the countryside was rudely disturbed by massive construction work with the building of the Mossford Reservoir. Scotland certainly isn't short of rivers or lochs to take all this rain that keeps pouring down. At times it's so persistent I wonder if there's a plumbing problem up above!

Later in the afternoon we joined the A835 at Gorstan and turned north-easterly into the Garbat Forest but after four miles the road swung back to north-westerly, became more exposed and I found myself battling with a strong head wind. This wind continued for nearly eight miles along the coast of Loch Glascarnoch but had eased by the time I stopped for tea opposite little Loch Droma.

The final evening session was mainly downhill and the weather was marvellous. I suppose if we didn't have rain we wouldn't have this beautiful scenery but at last we were seeing a lot of heather. About 5 p.m. we reached the Braemore Forest, the Falls of Measach in the Corrieshalloch Gorge and some quite spectacular views. The day ended in the Lael Forest where we found a secluded parking place in a picnic area. Close by were three very large and tall Wellingtonian firs and at dusk we could see a thrush (Mavis in Scotland!) perched right on top of one of them. We watched, fascinated, through binoculars as he or she entertained us with song for nearly an hour. It was non-stop, at full volume, and I'm sure she only stopped because of a sore throat. I was delighted with a score of 43 miles and could see no reason why we shouldn't manage over 40 each day. At least that would be our serious target.

As I was drifting off to sleep thinking about that thrush and the beautiful Scottish forests I recalled the last verse of a famous poem:

I remember, I remember,
The fir trees dark and high,
I used to think their slender tops,
Were close against the sky:
It was a childish ignorance
But now 'tis little joy,
To know I'm further off from heaven,
Than when I was a boy.

With all these beautiful surroundings of nature and the wonderful gift of sight, we should always try and ...

Take Time To See

It seems so hard to understand

As I look out across the land
That all I view belongs to me,
I ought to take more time to see!

The distant hills and mountains high,
The rolling clouds and bright blue sky,
No one can take these views from me
As long as I have eyes to see.

A timid deer with haunting look
Who stands refreshed by yonder brook
Knows not that he belongs to me,
Oh, what a thrilling sight to see!

The song of birds so gay and clear
That fill the morning air with cheer
And fragrant flowers of every hue
That stand erect bedecked with dew,
All these and more belong to me
If I but use my eyes to see.

When evening shadows gather nigh
And twinkling stars light up the sky
I hear my master say to me
'I made it all for you to see'.
My heart grows warm with faith and pride
To know that He is by my side.

Friday I was on the road by 6.20. It was another cold and overcast day but at least it was dry. My starting point was actually a couple of miles beyond our camp site and before very long I was running alongside Loch Broom—a sea loch—and heading for Ullapool. I reached this little port soon after breakfast. The British Fisheries Society built Ullapool in 1788. The string of low, whitewashed fisher cottages along the harbour road are still there though renovated to modern standards. The herring fishing in the Minch (the passage between the mainland and the western isles) has been a lavish source of food for nearly 300 years but it has declined in recent years. Holiday traffic has increased considerably with the introduction in 1974 of a car ferry from Ullapool to Stornoway on the Isle of Lewis.

9 Racing for the Kylesku ferry: 15 miles to go!

Ullapool, with its population of around 1,000 is the last place of any size on the road to the north of Scotland. I left Megan window and grocery shopping and set off back into the mountains and the endless journey northwards. Within minutes the rain was back to torment me and I began to wonder when we would next encounter a full day of normal sunshine. Every time we listened to the news we got the impression that the whole of the British Isles, except the Davids and their caravan, were basking in a heatwave.

We stopped for lunch at a location marked as Knockanrock which was opposite a tiny, wee loch. There was also a nature reserve called Inverpolly and not far away we could see there was a pot-holing centre. The weather pattern was much the same as yesterday, with the rain easing in the afternoon, but at the same time a head wind sprung up. Hopefully, when we reached Durness and started to run eastwards the wind would be back to westerly and then begin to help more rather than hinder.

By 3 p.m. I had reached a point called Ledmore Junction where I joined the A837, 15 miles south of the Kylesku ferry, with four hours remaining before the last ferry sailed. We didn't want to miss that last crossing, so we stopped for a short tea break before embarking on the final session. It was just as we reached Ledmore Junction that a car pulled up and the woman driver insisted on giving me a £1 coin to put in our charity box.

This was a very deserted and quiet area but I seemed to be running quite well, reaching the southern tip of Loch Assynt before 5 p.m. The stark ruins of Ardvreck Castle could be seen on a peninsula near the eastern end of the loch. The marquess of Montrose was imprisoned here in 1650 before being taken to Edinburgh and execution.

Soon after passing the castle I turned right onto the A894 and immediately climbed very steeply into the Highland range between two large peaks and was, again, rewarded with spectacular views. I was tiring by the time I reached the top and it's surprising how cold it can be at several thousand feet even in June. However, the last three miles were all downhill and we reached Unapool and the Kylesku ferry well before 7 p.m. The crossing itself only took 20 minutes and we were interested to hear that the Queen was due in a fortnight to open a new bridge that would make the ferry obsolete.

The road on the other side was very narrow with no prospect of any reasonable parking spot. Eventually, after about two miles, we parked for the night in a special scenic view spot overlooking Eddrachillis Bay and the Minch. We couldn't have had a better view of the sea but we took extra care to see that the brakes were fully on as we were parked on the edge of a cliff.

Quite a successful run as we had managed to achieve over 40 miles by just one mile.

Saturday was the last day of June and, hopefully, the last day that we would be heading on a mainly northerly course. This was going to be a shorter run of 33 miles as we planned to have a rest night in a hotel or guesthouse when we reached our destination of Durness. Judging by the AA books and our caravan touring maps this was going to be a worrying day for Megan. Ahead of us were some very steep and very narrow roads, not really suitable for towing caravans. We made a slightly earlier start at 6.10. In these latitudes it was light very early in the morning and very late at night.

I'd only gone four miles before I came across the first very steep, narrow and twisting hill that was also situated on the edge of a cliff. It was with great relief that I reached the top and found Megan safely parked and cooking breakfast. She told me very firmly that she wasn't very anxious to tackle any more similar obstacles, but she did, and I felt a bit of a coward at taking the easier route.

The scenery was very stark and, at times, I thought I was running on the barren mountains of the moon. There was not much heather or greenery. It was mainly rock. Plenty of sandpipers and several stonechats were amongst the gorse bushes. The landscape was completely different from anything I'd seen in Wales or Dartmoor and at times I felt as though I was on another planet.

By 11 a.m. we had negotiated several more very steep and narrow hills and each time I reached the top I was relieved to see Megan parked somewhere near at hand. These roads were so narrow that it was necessary to cut passing points every 400 yards. It must have been very worrying for her, driving up these steep slopes, praying that another vehicle wouldn't appear from the other direction or compel her to stop half way up the gradient. It would have been impossible to restart again. Fortunately there were hardly any vehicles and we didn't see anyone working on the land all day, even though there was a lot of peat already cut and presumably lying out to dry.

The last of the steep hills ended soon after passing through the little village of Scourie and after that it was a fairly easy run to Laxford Bridge where we joined the A838 from Lairg on Scotland's east coast. We climbed for about a mile from this point with a wonderful view overlooking the North Minch and Loch Laxford, which is a seawater loch.

Just before lunch, near the hamlet of Rhiconich, an ambulance and an RAF Mountain Rescue vehicle sped past me down a narrow turning marked 'Venture School', run by the explorer John Ridgway, so I hoped there hadn't been a serious accident.

After lunch it looked a fairly straight run all the way to Durness, which we hoped to reach by 5 p.m. Late in the afternoon I caught up with Megan who had pulled in at one of the passing points and was making a cup of tea. Either side of the road the coarse grass, bog land and boulder strewn landscape stretched for miles until it reached the mountains. We appeared to be on a high plateau of this wet and soggy peat land. We let Merlin loose to have a run and she immediately disturbed a redshank and set off in pursuit, reaching overdrive as she disappeared out of sight. Normally she would not venture further than a radius of about 200 yards before returning to base, but lately she had worried us by extending her limits quite considerably. Today was going to be an exception because within minutes she was out of sight and had shown no signs of circling back towards us. We quickly scanned the crest of the hill over which she had run, but there

10 The last day's crossing. We caught it!

was no sign of her and we were worried that she might lose her sense of direction if she ventured too far. There wasn't a soul in sight apart from some sheep on the edge of the mountain range, which was over a mile away. After ten minutes the stillness and quietness was quite eerie and Megan was almost in a state of panic. I told her to stay by the caravan while I set off across the plateau in the direction in which I'd last seen the dog. We both had binoculars and she promised not to follow me but to sound the horn if the dog returned. I was apprehensive about running into a bog, as I knew they could be very dangerous and deceptive in moorland areas, and I had to tread carefully and often jump from tuft to tuft. Occasionally I was frightened when the ground felt quite spongy and soft.

I reached the crest after half a mile and I stopped to sweep the exposed view with my binoculars, but there was no sign of Merlin. The feeling of loss was dreadful and I felt certain she must have drowned somewhere in a bog or, alternatively, got totally lost and was running into the barren mountain landscape miles away.

It was now nearly an hour since we had last seen her and I realised I must return to Megan who would be very upset. I didn't want her wandering into this dangerous peat bog plateau. I decided to scan the horizon once more and then, suddenly, over a mile away, I could see a white speck running near the foot of the mountain range. It was too far to be certain, although I was overjoyed with confidence that it must be Merlin, but when I looked again all I could see was a circling buzzard and no other sign of life.

I was now surrounded by odd pools of water and yellow spongy moss and I dared not go any further, so I quickly and very carefully retraced my footsteps back to the caravan. I told Megan that I thought I had spotted Merlin heading for the mountains, so we decided to unhitch the caravan and leave the door open, drive into Durness and see if we could muster some sort of rescue service. Then, suddenly, I spotted Merlin running up the road towards us, soaked in peat coloured water, looking totally exhausted but wagging her tail so hard I thought she'd do herself an injury. She'd been such good company and we would have been heartbroken if we had lost her in this northerly wasteland of Britain.

I left Megan drying the dog and, I suspect, feeding her with bread, milk and a drop of brandy, while I tackled the remaining seven or eight miles to Durness. Megan told me that a young couple, touring on bicycles, had arrived on the scene when I was absent on the plateau and had kindly waited until they saw me returning. I was so elated that the afternoon drama had ended happily that, for the next few miles, I felt as though I was running on cloud nine. Never again would we allow Merlin such uncontrolled freedom.

Almost immediately after this episode I saw a weasel by the roadside and she was quite tame, standing on her back legs with her ears pointing forwards. She was corn coloured with a white front and as thin as a pencil. When I got too close I saw her run off the road and she popped into a hole in the bank of a nearby stream.

The last few miles I was running alongside the tidal waters of Kyle of Durness with its large variety of birds and golden sands. As I began to leave this inlet I saw the rough minor road signposted to Cape Wrath, the extreme north-westerly point of Scotland. If we had arrived earlier I had hoped to drive out to this cape to see where one of the Clan Line steamers had run aground in a winter's storm in the 1950s.

I finally reached Durness about 6 p.m. and, after a few enquiries we booked into Mrs Ross's West End guest house. We had a most enjoyable supper and, after a few phone calls and a hot bath, I retired to bed. Not a great score—only 33 miles—but at least we'd arrived at the most north westerly village in Britain.

Sunday morning breakfast was arranged for 9 so I decided to get up at 7 and cover about five miles on our new easterly course across the roof of Scotland before returning to the guest house for a quick bath and a bacon and egg breakfast. Before leaving the house I reset the alarm clock which would give Megan an extra half hour's sleep before she needed to set off on my trail to bring me back to Durness.

It was yet another overcast and drizzly morning, but not too uncomfortable, and I actually managed to run or walk six miles before Megan caught up with me.

It was interesting to note that around the village of Durness there was a considerable amount of grass and less heather and far fewer stones and boulders, for the basic rock there was an outcrop of Durness Limestone. Six miles east of the village it returned to the bare rockery landscape.

At breakfast an elderly couple from the Borders area recognised me and said they had passed me near Eilean Donan Castle, about 150 miles south, which goes to show that there can not be many interesting sights on the roads of Scotland!

We thanked Mrs Ross for her kindness and hospitality and, after hitching on the caravan, we left Durness, with its small crofts, at 10.30 thinking that I wouldn't like to gamble on a business based on tourism in such a remote area.

For most of the day I had to run three-quarters of the way round Loch Eriboll on a road not really suitable for the caravan. At one point Megan met a van where there was insufficient passing room and the driver of the van insisted on taking over from Megan and reversing our car and caravan. Megan thought he was going to strip our gearbox. By the time I arrived the panic was over and I could see Megan about a mile away negotiating a very steep hill with a sheer drop into the loch below. I kept my eyes firmly focused on the distant crest of the hill as I jogged along hoping no vehicle would appear from the other direction. It was our lucky day and I was relieved when I saw Megan dip out of view on the other side. Running (or driving) in Scotland was never boring. The terrain, however, was very difficult to run on. There were so many twists and turns and the hills were so steep, whether up or down. The scenery is a mixture of desolation and beauty and at times it's like running on the roof of the world with mountain tops all around as far as your eyes can see. They are almost at your own level and mostly shrouded in mist and cloud and, apart from the wild birds, there is a feeling of loneliness and depression.

Later in the afternoon the sun popped out as I was descending from this remote region to sea level and Tongue Bay where I crossed a very long bridge spanning the Kyle of Tongue. This deserted north coast had some very attractive beaches. One particularly beautiful one was Coldbackie with nearly a mile of golden sands.

Soon after running through this hamlet I caught up with Megan and for the first time for many days I was feeling very hot, so I took off my Macmillan Cancer Relief Fund singlet and put it on the car roof while drinking a glass of lemonade. After a short break I set off, without my vest, but it wasn't until later, when I was cold, that I realised that it must have fallen off the car roof and Megan had to find me another one. It was some two hours later, when I was running down a long incline, a lone cyclist overtook me and without saying a word he reached into his saddlebag, pulled out my vest and just dropped it on the road about 100 yards ahead! Like most of the tourists in this area, I think he was probably a continental!

A few miles further on, in the Borgie Forest, we found our campsite for the night. Shopping was a little difficult in this neck of the woods as papers, milk and bread are not delivered until late afternoon. Weekends are extra difficult. So instead of baked beans on toast it was biscuits—and the milk was rationed. Our nearest shopping point was possibly Thurso which was still some 30 miles away. The day's run was 39 miles.

Monday morning, 2 July, I made a slightly earlier start after helping myself to the usual plate of cornflakes and glass of milk. I was on the road by 6.10. It was overcast, mild and no rain or drizzle. Within the hour I was running through the little village of Bettyhill which looked as though it was suffering from an epidemic of rabbits! Never in my life have I seen so many. They were on the roads, in the gardens and in one field I guessed there were at least 200 of them, including a black one. Most of Scotland, and parts of the east coast of England, appeared to have an over population of rabbits, but this village's problems looked exceptional.

Bettyhill was just half a mile from the sea, and here too were large stretches of golden sands but little evidence of any holidaymakers. These rural villages are not particularly attractive. The houses are spread out, in need of repair and have a general air of depression and poverty. They look more like settlements than villages.

The morning's run was quite uneventful, with the road running on

11 Merlin pacing me in the hills of Sutherland.

a high plateau about a mile south of the coast, until I reached a particularly lonely spot where the road ran close to a tern colony's breeding ground. All of a sudden I realised that several of these birds were actually trying to attack me as I ran by. At first I was amused, until one whistled past my ear screaming something very unpleasant in bird language. I was no longer amused and began to feel decidedly apprehensive as the attacks continued. I stopped running and walked briskly until things quietened down. When I finally reached the caravan I thought Megan wouldn't believe such an unlikely story, so I looked up 'Tern' in the *AA Book of British Birds*, which stated: 'Both of these birds are intensely aggressive at their breeding colonies. They dive bomb intruders, screaming their anger with harsh cries of "Keeyah", and have been known to draw blood from a man's head'. I don't know whether these birds were the common tern or the Arctic tern, but the paragraph applies to both of them. When not angry, these birds have a very unusual, slow, gentle and graceful flight and are often referred to as the swallows of the sea. So beware of the tern unless you are running with a crash helmet.

We finally stopped for lunch immediately opposite the Dounreay Atomic Fast Reactor which looked so small that at first we didn't realise where we were. This was Britain's first prototype fast breeder reactor, built in 1956. The site is not open to the public.

The landscape had changed quite suddenly in the last few miles and we were aware of civilisation again with green fields and cattle grazing alongside the reactor. We didn't stay too long because we had merely pulled in to the side of the road and were not actually in a lay-by. It was just eight miles to Thurso and Megan agreed to go on ahead. We arranged to meet each other at 4.30 p.m. at the main post office.

It was a pleasant, cool, sunny afternoon and quite perfect for running. I stopped for a rest at a beauty spot called 'Bridge of Forss' where there was a salmon leap, and enjoyed an ice cream which I had purchased from the small post office stores as I watched the river Forss completing its journey to the sea from Loch Calder in the Highlands.

The next two miles were uphill but the last three were downhill all the way into Thurso, the most northerly town on the British mainland, which I reached just after 4.15. I met Megan at the post office and, after a quick look at the shopping centre, we returned to the caravan to enjoy tea with fresh cakes. Near the harbour are some well restored houses dating from the seventeenth and eighteenth centuries and the ruins of St Peter's church stand on a site occupied since the days of the Vikings.

By 5 o'clock I was jogging out of Thurso en route for the village of Dunnet where we planned to make camp for the night. I was quite tired when I reached the village of Castletown. I didn't seem to have my usual evening's reserve of energy. However, I didn't want to get behind schedule so, after a short break, I continued the final stage of three miles to the village of Dunnet. The road route between these two villages runs alongside Dunnet Bay with three glorious miles of sandy beaches. What a waste that there isn't more sunshine, warmth and people to enjoy it.

At Dunnet we left the main road and followed the A855 for about a mile where we found a suitable pull-in for the night. This road would lead us directly to Dunnet Head and the lighthouse. It was my best day's run of 44 miles so perhaps I was entitled to feel tired.

It was a cold night and, for some reason, I didn't sleep very well. Every time I woke up it still appeared to be quite light outside. I don't think they have more than a couple of hours of darkness in these high latitudes at this time of the year but it doesn't really feel like summer weather. We had now reached a stage where we could forecast our future destinations quite accurately. It was fairly simple to calculate on an average day's run of 40 miles, which I felt I could now maintain without any particular difficulties.

As usual, I was awake before dawn, and by 6.20 we had disconnected the caravan and I was striding out to complete the three miles separating me from the most northerly point of mainland Britain. It was exactly 7 p.m. when I reached Dunnet Head which is crowned by a lighthouse that, though standing 100 metres above the sea, is liable to have its windows shattered by stones hurled up in the fierce winter storms of the Pentland Firth, one of the roughest stretches of sea in Europe. It was a clear, overcast morning and there were magnificent views eight miles across the Firth to the 'Old Man of Hoy' in the Orkney Islands, the island of Stroma and large sections of Scotland's northern shoreline. Strong tides of ten knots race through the Pentland Firth and to steam through it on a dark and stormy winter's night in an old 10,000-ton 'Empire Boat' with maximum speed of 10 knots could be quite interesting! For hours progress might be nil as the 10-knot ship battled against the 10-knot current — but once the tide turned the ship was suddenly progressing at 20 knots. In poor visibility it was sometimes difficult to know whether the ship was progressing at 0 or 20 knots. Tide tables, giving the times of high tide and low tide, are not very reliable in stormy weather.

Before leaving the area we took a few photographs and looked over the cliffs to see if we could see any puffins, but we were out of luck. I didn't need to run all the way back to the village of Dunnet but took another minor road north, off St John's Loch, rejoining the main road several miles east of Dunnet. We stopped beyond the village of Mey, disconnected the caravan, and drove down a side road to see how close we could get to the Castle of Mey, favourite holiday home of the late Queen Mother. The castle is situated half way between Dunnet Head and John O'Groats. We didn't get very close and had to satisfy ourselves with a view from our binoculars. Sadly we were not invited in for morning coffee!

After reconnecting the caravan, Megan drove ahead and agreed to wait for me at John O'Groats, which was about five miles further on. No sooner had Megan left than it started to drizzle and it became quite cold but, with only five miles to go and the thought of hot soup, I was soon scorching along at 8 7mph. I reached John O'Groats at noon and decided it was a very disappointing and unattractive spot. Just a few cottages and the inevitable souvenir places. There were

12 John O'Groats at last. It's all downhill from here!

hardly any visitors so, after taking a few photographs, I was happy to return to the caravan and enjoy lunch. In fairness, I'm certain we would have been far more enthusiastic if it had been a fine, hot summer's day and would have enjoyed the coastal views to Duncansby Head and across Gills Bay towards the Castle of Mey.

I had now run a total of 1,414 miles since leaving Wool and 1,190 miles from Land's End. The shortest distance from Land's End to John O'Groats is 879 miles, but my route had included South Wales. It was nice to realise that I was well over half way and from now on our course would be in a southerly direction.

During the lunch hour we had been studying the maps and I had failed to convince myself that it was now all downhill to England. Unfortunately I'd spotted the Cairngorm Mountains and realised there were a few tough hurdles still ahead of us. However, I sensed a new spring in my step as I set off on this new southerly course, uphill from John O'Groats. The sun was ahead of me with a cool north westerly wind pushing me along.

11

Caithness to Newcastle
via the Cairngorms

We had now established a fairly regular routine in our general eating, living and my running habits. The average day would start with the alarm ringing at 5.30. I would get up, dress in the appropriate running gear to match the weather conditions, help myself to half a bowl of cornflakes, a glass of milk, reset the alarm for 6.30 and then start the day's run soon after 6. If we had parked some distance down a side road then Megan would get up too and drive me back to the 'start point' on the main route. We were, latterly, parking more often in the main road lay-bys as we had tended to waste so much time in the evenings looking for side road parking places. The disadvantage of the main road lay-bys was the noise of the night time traffic and, strictly speaking, you are not supposed to park in these lay-bys overnight.

This first morning session was usually five miles and most of that distance I jogged very easily. Megan would get up at 6.30, take Merlin for a walk, then set off in my direction and look for a parking spot for breakfast after passing me and clocking a minimum of five miles.

Breakfast—or, for me, second breakfast—was half a grapefruit, toast and marmalade, a glass of milk or cup of tea. We tried to fit in a meeting point mid morning, when I'd require some sort of drink and, depending on the weather, it would be lemonade, Bovril, milk or tea.

We liked to listen to the 'News and Comments' at 1 p.m. so, whenever possible, Megan would calculate the best pull-in to meet this requirement. By this time I hoped to have run at least 20 miles and, after a lunch of cold meat, salad, cheese, biscuits and fruit, I would put my feet up and attempt to relax, or at least rest. As well as eating and resting we would generally use this period to study the maps and plan the rest of the day's route. Often I would also spend some time repairing my shoes by building up the worn heels with a rubberised liquid solution called 'Shoo-Goo'. I found it excellent, and it must have saved me quite a lot of money on shoe repairs.

The lunch break was usually 1¼–1½ hours. I then looked forward to tea, cake or sandwiches at about 4 p.m. which left, after a short rest, a final running session of about two hours. The day's run would end about 7 with supper at 8 and bed at 10. The average day's run was now about 40 miles and equally divided between 20 miles before lunch and the other 20 in the afternoon session. For supper Megan usually managed to cook fish or chops in the small stove. After supper we generally had telephone calls to make and would some-times pop into the local for a shandy. I didn't feel I was eating any more than my normal amount, but I was drinking vast amounts of lemonade, orange juice, milk, tea and shandy in the evenings.

It was a steady climb from John O'Groats, but it levelled out after a couple of miles and I was then able to enjoy several hours of easy, relaxed running, with a following breeze to help me along a little. An amusing incident occurred during the early afternoon which upset my steady running and concentration and could possibly have had more serious consequences. All of a sudden, ahead of me, I had spotted a snake by the edge of the road, which appeared to be motionless. On close inspection I realised that it was an adder and that a car wheel had squashed and flattened its middle section, but its front 6 inches and back 6 inches were round and very much alive! I got the impression that it was unable to move and was pinned to the road. I thought the kindest thing to do would be to put it out of its misery but I couldn't find any large stones or a stick to carry out the execution. Without remembering to engage my brain, I decided to stamp on it with my foot! I stood close to the snake, raised my right foot, took aim and jabbed quickly at the animal's head. My foot jarred as it hit the ground, the snake's head had moved quicker than lightening and, to my horror, was within an inch of my left ankle. It then seemed an appropriate moment to vacate that particularly isolated part of Britain and to run what was possibly my fastest mile! My eldest brother, Robin, always told me that I was guilty of engaging my brain last instead of giving it the priority it sadly needed!

It was late in the afternoon that I eventually reached Wick and, as previously arranged, met Megan at the main post office where we collected some mail that had been addressed to us c/o Wick Post Office. We spent half an hour buying stores and postcards and visiting the editor of the *Caithness Journal* who had written an article on our journey to date.

It was now a lovely sunny afternoon and we enjoyed a late tea and fresh cakes just the other side of town. My last session was a little tiring as it was a gradual uphill run against a gentle head wind. We camped about a mile off the main road, just beyond a small village called Thrumster. We were a little under our 40-mile target with a score of 37.

Wednesday 4 July I was back on the road at my usual time, hoping to make up a few miles on yesterday. This east coast of Scotland was more populated than the west but there were still too many derelict crofts and other abandoned properties. The rabbit population was almost unbelievable. The fields appeared to be crawling with them and, in the pre-breakfast session, I saw two black ones in the one field. I wondered if rabbits have 'colour' problems! It's odd what you think about when running for 12 hours a day.

We were following a very hilly coastal route with wonderful views out to sea. It was overcast and cool, but I found it very tiring as the hills were particularly steep. For reasons I didn't understand, it seemed that about every third day I felt more tired than usual, quite regardless of the road or weather conditions. I found it quite useful to have a definite aim and then set myself a target to achieve regardless of outside influences. I had already accepted that a 40-mile day should be a normal calculation.

Megan found a lovely parking spot for breakfast, on a high cliff overlooking the sea, with a southerly view as far as the Moray Firth. The road continued to follow the coastline but became steeper and narrower after passing through Lybster and Latheron. Some of the hairpin bends and very steep gradients began to worry me, particularly when by 11 a.m. Megan hadn't overtaken me since I had left the caravan at 9. after breakfast. By noon I was really worried and, as a result, had slowed down considerably and found myself continually looking backwards. Eventually, at about 12.30, Megan overtook me on yet another long, steep hill, but it was nearly another five miles before she could find a suitable lay-by. As a result, it was a 1.30 lunch. I felt very thirsty and exhausted and, in fact, fell asleep and didn't start my afternoon session until nearly 3. I very rarely allowed myself the luxury of 40 winks at any time of the day.

Megan had been delayed in the morning when she had stopped to replenish our water supplies. A Mrs Budge had kept her chatting and, before Megan left, she not only had her water container filled but was given a generous supply of homemade cakes and a jar of rhubarb jam.

Shortly before 4 p.m. I caught up with Megan again. She was parked at one of those special 'Principal Island Viewpoints' with panoramic views into the North Sea and the coastline running both north and south. Suddenly the sun came out and it became quite warm so I took the opportunity to change back into shorts for the first time in over two weeks.

It was all downhill for the next three miles, into the village of Helmsdale, with a couple of very steep hills with sharp bends, but that would end the difficult stretch for the caravan. The downhill run gave me my second wind so I didn't stop for tea until we reached the other side and then we found a parking spot close to a very sandy beach. This small fishing village of Helmsdale is at the foot of the valley of Kildonan. Until recently the remains of a castle built in 1488 stood on a headland above the village. It was the scene of the poisoning of the earl and countess of Sutherland in 1567, but the castle has now been completely demolished. However, a few miles up the Kildonan Valley are dozens of reminders of earlier cultures—standing stones, stone circles and cairns—on the moors on each side of the valley. It is quite clear that this area was quite well inhabited for some hundreds of years BC. Few of the remains are notable in themselves, but the sheer number of them is impressive. I realised that we were rapidly leaving the wilder and lonelier sections of Scotland and returning to green fields and arable farm land. I would miss the sandpipers, with their funny flight, the curlews and the oystercatchers. No doubt we would be back amongst some of them again when we approached the Cairngorms.

The late run was a lovely summer's evening and took me through the small coastal resort of Brora, with its sands and golf course. I finally stopped at 7.30 a mile north east of Dunrobin Castle. This was a record day's run of 45 miles which earned me a couple of shandies!

Before 6.30 on 5 July I was jogging past Dunrobin Castle, the ancient seat of the earls and dukes of Sutherland since the thirteenth century. The castle's present appearance dates from mid nineteenth-century extensions, but the core of this architectural extravagance is a tower built in 1275. The local village of Golspie was still asleep, with the exception of a milk delivery van, which seemed to me to be early for this part of the world.

It was level and fairly easy running and Megan found an excellent pull-in for breakfast, right on the shores of Loch Fleet. I'd only just set off on the after breakfast session when I met two enthusiasts heading north to John O'Groats on penny farthing bicycles. They were very well organised, with a special Land Rover back-up vehicle, and we did manage to exchange a few humourous remarks and wish each other a safe journey. I'd seen their venture mentioned in the *Caithness Journal* and hoped we might meet somewhere en route.

By 11 a.m. I was running inland along the north shore of the Dornoch Firth, through Clashmore Wood and on to Bonar Bridge where we crossed over the water and headed seaward along the southerly shore. It was a warm, beautiful, sunny day and a change from the wilderness of Scotland's far north to the tranquil pastureland surrounding this estuary. Halfway along this southern shore we decided to leave the A9 and take a short cut through the mountains of eastern Ross on the A836. The caravan route map gave it the OK, but there was one very long and steep climb up from the estuary, which was at sea level. It took nearly 1½ hours to walk to the top of this mountain range (except for a few odd stretches, running was impossible), but when I did, there was another one of those special parking areas where there were breathtaking views of Dornoch Firth to the north and Cromarty Firth and Moray Firth to the south. I think, too, I could see the towns of Dingwall and Inverness. It was an ideal spot to enjoy afternoon tea and allow the car to cool down. Also resting were a group of ordinary racing cyclists who were heading for John O'Groats from Land's End. I can not remember their figures, but I was astonished at the speeds they were travelling. My effort seemed to be insignificant compared to theirs. I was lucky to run the final session mainly downhill, finding a lay-by on a short loop road at Evanton. After supper I telephoned an Inverness newspaper, who wanted to interview us, and arranged an appointment for the following morning. I went to bed feeling quite satisfied with the day's run of 43 miles.

On Friday 6 July we were up early and I was on the road very soon after 6 a.m. with the weather mild but overcast. Within a few minutes I was stopped by quite a young woman who was obviously much the worse for alcohol. It was a very odd hour to be hitting the bottle!

The bridge spanning the Cromarty Firth must have been nearly two miles in length and, soon after crossing it, I caught up with Megan who had breakfast waiting for me. By 9 a.m. I had already covered ten miles and for the first time for two weeks I was back running on a dual carriageway, and not enjoying it. This one had a very narrow hard shoulder and the heavy traffic was not impressed by my presence. Several overtook me too close for comfort and shaking a fist at them only helped to relieve my anger and frustration. Fortunately none of them stopped to take up my challenge!

I entered Inverness after crossing the Kessock Bridge, which spans the Moray Firth, and met Megan near the outskirts of the town where we managed to park the car and caravan. Inverness, often referred to as the capital of the Highlands, has a magnificent setting where the roads from Fort William, the Spey Valley, the Moray coast and the north and west Highlands meet. The first documentary evidence of a settlement comes from St Adamnan's account of St Columba coming to King Brude in AD 565 to seek his approval for monks from Iona to preach Christianity to the Picts. It has a wonderful scenic setting and stands on both sides of the river Ness with salmon and trout fishing in the middle of the town! Inverness is the Highland's major touring centre and Loch Ness is less than seven miles south-west of the town.

After calling at the newspaper offices we did some shopping, but gave up after half an hour as the town was too crowded and I couldn't afford to lose too much time. We stopped for lunch a few miles east of Inverness and about three miles south of Culloden Moor. Here, in 1746, the last battle to be fought in the United Kingdom took place between Bonnie Prince Charlie's Jacobites and a Hanoverian army under the duke of Cumberland. One of the world's greatest romances came to grief in this battle, which only lasted 40 minutes. From the moment he landed in Scotland until he escaped 14 months later, as a bedraggled fugitive, from the mountains of the Hebrides, this daring young man had attempted to replace his father, a Stuart, on the throne of England. Culloden is one of the very few battlefields in the world which contains the graves of the fallen, buried in trenches where they died. Waterloo is a place of farms, the Ypres Salient is obliterated by crops, and on Hell Fire Corner stands a little new house with a washing line. The sadness of Culloden Moor can still be felt with the weatherworn stones rising from the heath with the names of Highland clans who died for the Stuarts. Such names as

Clan McGillivray, MacClean, MacLachlan, Stewarts, Cameron and Mackintosh. (As a Welshman I had actually sailed on Clan Line ships bearing all these different names.)

The battle took place on the 16 April in a freezing north-easterly gale with rain and sleet blowing straight into the faces of Bonnie Prince Charlie and his waiting Jacobite Army. The Jacobites were outnumbered two to one and stood little or no chance at all. They were blinded by their own gunsmoke and were soon cut to pieces by the opposing army. It was a heroic waste of lives and men. An estimated 1,200 Highlanders and 364 Hanoverian soldiers were killed in this brief encounter. Cumberland's senseless cruelty in killing the wounded and the prisoners earned him the name of 'Butcher'. It was the loyalty of the Highland people, who hid and sheltered their prince, that enabled him to eventually escape from Scotland.

After lunch I was back in my weatherproof outfit with the rain pouring down. It wasn't a good day for running. I felt tired for most of the time and, although the heavy rain stopped, showers continued on and off all day. The main road, the A9, from Inverness to Perth, was quite busy but the traffic didn't worry me like it had on the dual carriageway. One amazing aspect of this particular section of road was the kerb stones. Each stone was about 18 inches long and, for some reason, it had a small ridge at one end sticking out about an inch. I always ran very close to the edge of these roads and, with this silly little ridge, I kept brushing it with my right shoe (running against the traffic). Late in the afternoon the inevitable happened. I was running downhill and quite fast when suddenly, through tiredness and lack of concentration, I touched the edge of the kerb stone, tripped and fell quite heavily. Luckily no damage was done, but my outstretched hand was very close to a broken beer bottle. That was to be the only time I tripped or fell in over 2,000 miles!

The last five miles were all uphill and I felt very tired by the time we found our lovely parking spot. I was very pleased to put my feet up and 'call it a day'. I was exhausted but delighted with a score of 41 miles. We were back in the mountains!

The previous night we had camped just off the A9 on the A938. This Saturday morning I was actually on the run before 6 a.m. and we were following a secondary road which, within 20 minutes, brought me into the small village of Carrbridge. We were now in the centre of the Highland holiday resorts and this small village has one of the finest visitor centres in Europe. Unfortunately, we didn't have time to see it but I understand it has an exciting audio-visual display that covers some 10,000 years of history. The road through the village has a bridge crossing the river Dulnain, but alongside it is another beautiful old bridge, with a picturesque arch, built in 1715 by the earl of Seafield for the use of funeral parties going to Duthil on the road to Dulnain Bridge. It was really beautiful countryside with the high peaks of Cairngorm and Ben Avon just over 19 miles to the south. I was running with forests on either side of me and, suddenly, I saw a red squirrel in one of the firs. I just stopped and watched him playing in the branches—I hadn't seen one for 40 years! It was still quite early morning, and within another ten minutes a doe deer sneaked across the road in front of me.

I met Megan at a petrol station in Aviemore and she agreed to stop for a late breakfast as soon as we'd cleared the town. Aviemore looked very modern, very expensive and obviously geared up to skiing holidays.

I was now running on the A9152 which was parallel to and about a quarter of a mile from the A9. Following the river Spey I passed little Loch Insh, the Highland Wildlife Park, and rejoined the main A9 road a mile east of Kingussie. For the next five miles we had a choice of two routes and we decided to opt for the southerly one but, fortunately, as I watched Megan disappear, I realised she had turned off on the other route. When she became aware of her error she turned around at the first opportunity and was surprised to see me running towards her. It was again difficult to run much of this last 15-mile session as it was mostly uphill and with a fairly strong head wind. We parked for the night at Drumochter Summit which was not far from Dalwhinnie, the highest village in the Highlands. In the last mile I picked up a dead Sparrow Hawk which I guessed must have been hit by a speeding car as it skimmed across the road in pursuit of its prey. I was surprised how small it was. It had quite a sharp curved beak and very substantial talons.

Before going to bed I took Merlin for a long walk in the heather hoping we might see a covey of grouse or some other wildlife, but we didn't see anything of interest. I had intended making several phone calls but we came to the conclusion that the nearest telephone box was probably ten miles away, so we went to bed early satisfied with our 40-mile run.

I made a prompt start at 6 a.m. on Sunday morning, 8 July. It looked like being a lovely day as there was hardly any breeze, a clear

blue sky and the road was sloping gently downhill. We were still on
very high ground but from this point we were beginning our descent
out of the Grampian Mountains down the Garry Valley. Well below
me, on my right, was the river Garry, and on my left was the Forest
of Atholl. About 7 a.m. I disturbed a blackcock (black grouse) and as
he flew out of the young fir trees across the road in front of me I
could see his distinctive lyre shaped tail. That was the only black or
red grouse that we saw in either Scotland or Yorkshire. It would have
been a special thrill if we'd seen a 17 lb capercaillie! Not long after
seeing the blackcock I spotted a buck, doe and two baby deer on the
far side of the valley, out for a morning stroll.

Mid morning we took a secondary road running parallel to the
main route but a much prettier way passing Blair Castle. This castle
was renovated at the end of the eighteenth century and turned into a
very attractive Georgian mansion. We spent about half an hour in the
little village, enjoying an ice cream, before heading south again.

There were some wonderful and spectacular views as I ran through
Killiecrankie and alongside the steep and narrow gorge where the
river Tummel rushes southwards to join the river Tay. I stopped for
a quick drink at Pitlochry and then continued for another three miles
and, soon after rejoining the main A9 road, we stopped for lunch.
While resting and reading tit-bits about the area, I came across this
amusing story concerning a church in the village of Meigle, about 20
miles to the east of Pitlochry. It's an account sent out to the minister
by one J. Jones, a joiner, for services rendered:

REV. J MAQUIRE   Nov. 1st, 1605

To J JONES, JOINER

For solidly rendering St Joseph	£0-0-4
Cleaning and repairing Holy Ghost	£0-0-6
Repairing Mary behind and before,	
And making her a new child	£0-5-6
To making a nose to the devil	
And fitting a horn on his head	
And giving a piece to his tail	£0-6-6
	£0-12-10

13 Resting with Merlin at Blair Atholl.

Mr Jones sounds like a very precise and careful Welshman!

It was a very pleasant, warm and sunny afternoon as I continued my run through the Tay Valley. The gently sloping valley was leading me down and out of the Highlands, passing Craigvinean Forest, the Hermitage, and eventually into greener pasture lands. I had been following the river Tay for most of the afternoon, but about 5 p.m. I diverted onto the B867 which took me through Waterloo and Bankfoot before again rejoining the A9 and the Strathord Forest an hour later. We found our camping site down a side road two miles west of the village of Stanley.

After supper we unhitched the caravan, drove into Perth six miles away, made some phone calls and stopped for a shandy before returning to base. Another good day's run of 45 miles.

Now that we were leaving the Highlands I was sorry that we had only once seen a herd of the shaggy Highland cattle, which was somewhere near Kyle of Lochalsh, or perhaps it was Ullapool. These docile cows, with their long, elegant, upturned horns and thick shaggy coats, are a very hardy breed. They can survive in very rough country with little hay or straw in the severest of winter conditions.

We were up quite early and I ran through the city of Perth around 7 a.m. with very little traffic to bother me. Unfortunately, our route through this fine city, set at the head of the Tay estuary, took us through the side streets, so we saw very little of interest and wished we'd seen the city centre.

Once clear of the city, we looked for the A912 which was the old route to the Forth Bridge, replaced in recent years by the M90 motorway. The A912 ran close to the M90 route but it was very quiet and we noticed that we had completely lost all trace of heather, rivers and mountains. The further south we progressed the richer the farmland became.

About mid morning, running alongside a wooded area, I came across a dead red squirrel, and I was surprised that it was such a small animal, weighing not more that 2 or 3 ounces.

We lunched about a mile beyond Loch Leven and were disappointed when the sun disappeared and rain clouds filled the sky. Fortunately, the rain held off, although it was quite cold. I made steady progress, with just a few minor hills and very little traffic. By late afternoon I was running on the B917 and heading rapidly towards the Forth Bridge. I caught up with Megan on the outskirts of Cowdenbeath and stopped for tea and also to plan the final session. A few miles further back I had stopped a police car and they told me that Megan could park on this northern side of the Forth Bridge and wait for me to arrive.

After tea we had arranged to meet at the bridge, but if anything should go wrong I put a £1 note in my pocket for emergencies and enough for toll payment, if required, and I knew Megan would stop at the first available lay-by en route to Edinburgh if she found the bridge parking spots were all full.

The last two or three miles to the bridge approach were quite unnerving. There was no hard shoulder at all, just a raised metal barrier to mark the full extent of the road area. There was no space on the other side of the barrier, only gorse, rock, rubbish and broken bottles. To make matters worse, I was running in the rush hour and, have you noticed how many drivers always seem to race to bridges or ferries! Another hazard was loose chippings from fallen pieces of overhanging rock. I had to watch my footsteps but couldn't do anything about one or two that whistled past me like bullets from lorry tyres! In the last mad mile race for the bridge (by this time I was racing too!) I was tooted at twice, once by a lorry and then by a Mercedes that glided by less than a foot from my shoulder. I do hope he looked in his mirror and could lip read!

Thankfully, Megan was parked close to the bridge so I was able to rest for about 20 minutes to unwind, have a rest and a drink before tackling the bridge. It was now 6 p.m., and we decided to get as close to Edinburgh as possible so that I could run through the city early next morning, before the rush hour. The rain clouds had disappeared and it was another lovely summer's evening as I ran across the Forth Bridge on the special outside section reserved for pedestrians and cyclists. I had a good view of Edinburgh and also the city's port, Leith. The last time I had been in Edinburgh was during that glorious summer of 1947 when I was a cadet on HMT *Clan Lamont*. It was a troopship, transporting Polish forces back to the port of Gdansk after the Second World War. If I remember correctly, the round voyage took eight days and we carried 1,600 troops. I was with the ship for about five months and it was like one long holiday with never-ending sunshine and no rough seas or storms. There was the magnificent scenery of the coastlines of Norway, Sweden and Denmark as we negotiated the Skagerrak and Kattegat, separating the North Sea from the Baltic Sea. The only sad memories were the welcoming party for the returning servicemen of Poland, which were cattle trucks, Russian soldiers armed with tommy guns and a handful of civilians beyond the dock area. We were not allowed ashore.

The Forth Bridge is over four miles in length, including the immediate approaches, which is something you notice if you are running over it. After crossing the bridge the road was quite straightforward with the traffic dying down, dual carriageway and plenty of hard shoulder area for safe running. I was now on the A90, heading straight for the city of Edinburgh, and wondering where we could possibly park that night. I thought it likely that, close to the city, we would be moved on by the police if we settled in at a dual carriageway lay-by. Luckily I caught up with Megan who was waiting in a lay-by and worrying about this particular problem when, at the bottom of the hill, I could see a pub. I ran on down the hill and the landlord very kindly gave his permission for us to park there overnight in his large car park. So, I waved Megan to come on and we manoeuvred the car and caravan into an out of the way spot where we could make a 4 a.m. escape the following morning. We felt very pleased with ourselves as we were now positioned exactly where we had planned—on the outskirts of the city—and in walking distance of a shandy! Another good day's run of 42 miles.

On Tuesday 10 July the dawn woke us at 4.30. In order to avoid the rush hour and not lose each other in the big city, we had decided on a 5 a.m. start. Although we were still in Scotland, I was amazed at the vast distance that we had travelled since we have arrived in Glasgow on Friday 22 June. It had taken me 18 days to run about 700 miles, at an average of 38 miles per day, over the north-west Highlands, through the desolate, windswept moors of Sutherland and Caithness and over the Cairngorm and Grampian mountain ranges to Perth and now, finally, Edinburgh.

As we approached the city centre the streets were almost deserted so Megan was able to keep in touch with me by kerb crawling. We nearly got into a muddle at one point, trying to follow the signs to Dalkeith, and Megan was disappointed that the one-way route system didn't take us down Princes Street. This street has been called the finest in the kingdom. There are shops on one side only. The other side runs along the edge of a deep ravine, planted with gardens, above which rises the Castle Rock and the high roofline of old Edinburgh.

Edinburgh is Scotland's finest city, and has been its capital since 1437. Its massive castle guards and overlooks this ancient city, with its history stretching back over a thousand years. When I reached the suburbs on the eastern side I was joined by a young lady who was out for her early morning run. She was interested in my adventure and kept me company for about four miles. I suddenly realised how much easier it was to run with a companion. Her name was Fiona Reading, and I hope I persuaded her to attempt one marathon in due course. She seemed to possess a very natural and easy running rhythm. We still exchange Christmas cards!

It was still only 7 a.m. when we stopped for breakfast near Dalkeith. By mid-morning I had cleared Pathhead and was heading into hill country again on the A68. It was uphill all the way to a little place called Oxton, where the road divided. Here we stopped for lunch and I was able to shelter from some fairly frequent showers.

Four miles after lunch I ran through the little country town of Lauder and the A68 was to follow the Leader river for another eight miles, through Earlston to Leaderfoot, where it joined the Tweed. The countryside was almost English with green pastures and acres of barley and wheat which were turning a golden colour. The weather was pleasant but not very warm. I had a very good afternoon's run and had reach Newtown St Boswells before stopping for tea and a rest. Not to put too fine a point on it, I was in need of a long soak in a hot bath, but realised I would have to settle for a lukewarm shower!

So, our last session was aimed at reaching the Lilliardsedge Caravan and Camping Park just a few miles north of Jedburgh. Megan went ahead to tackle the large bag of dirty washing and to order our evening meal, if possible, in the campsite. I found the last five miles quite tiring as it was rather hilly and I was struggling against a slight evening breeze. I was exhausted by the time I reached the camp, but had achieved my longest day's run of 47 miles. As expected, it was a lukewarm shower, which I felt I did not deserve. The supper they supplied wasn't much better, but I did sleep the moment my head hit the pillow.

We drove out of the camp slowly and quietly at 6 a.m., trying not to disturb the holidaymakers in adjacent tents and caravans. It was a clear, warm and sunny morning. There was still a lot of grass being cut and it was nice to smell the newly harvested hay. I got the impression that up north more grass is cut for hay than for silage, and this appears to be the reverse in England.

I caught up with Megan on the outskirts of Jedburgh where I found her buying milk from a delivery van. It was too early for the shops, but I took this opportunity to have an early breakfast and a quick sightseeing tour around the town. Jedburgh is a popular walking, climbing and riding centre, standing as a gateway to Scotland. Its finest attraction is the abbey, which is roofless and in ruins but nevertheless magnificent. It was one of King David I's Border abbeys and was burned by the English in 1523. Mary Queen of Scots is associated with the town and the sixteenth-century Mary Queen of Scots House incorporates a museum devoted to her life.

After our little tour and breakfast Megan drove on ahead of me with the intention of parking the caravan some five miles along the route and returning to the town to spend an hour on shopping and visiting some of the craft centres. It wasn't very long after I had left the town that the road began to meander upwards into the Cheviot Hills. By the time I found the caravan I was very thirsty and enjoyed the 20-minute break with my feet up. I then left before Megan

14 Mary, Megan and Philip at Gateshead.

returned from Jedburgh.

The route became very windy and steep as I approached the summit and huge black thunderclouds were overhead. It was now nearly
noon and I hoped Megan hadn't run into difficulty in reconnecting the
caravan after her shopping spree in Jedburgh. If she found it too
difficult I knew she could always come along and pick me up. It
started to pour with rain before I reached the top and there were
several bursts of thunder and lightning. I didn't have much option but
to carry on and hope it wouldn't last too long. It didn't, and the sun
came out as I reached the summit, called Carter Bar. Scotland meets
England at this 1,370-foot viewpoint in the Cheviot Hills. Lush
pastures and trim plantations spread out to the north, with the Eildon
Hills in the distance, and the Roman Camp and earthworks of Chew
Green lie to the east. At the summit viewpoint was the inevitable ice
cream van, several tour buses and a lone piper smartly dressed in his
kilt. Ahead of me, to the south, was a beautiful view of the lovely
tree clad Rede Valley and the Border Forest Park—and miles of
downhill to run!

I'd run about two miles into England before Megan finally caught
up with me. Unfortunately she had lost the spare caravan key so,

while she was making lunch, I disconnected the caravan and drove back into Scotland to look for the key at the previous parking site. I didn't find it.

It was a long and lonely run during the afternoon as I passed through the Redesdale Forest and then we followed close to the river Rede through open but wild country. We were still on quite a high plateau but we were descending very gradually. When I got to Otterburn I telephoned my niece in Newcastle and told her our current position. She said she would drive out to meet us later in the evening when we had eventually parked for the night.

At 7 p.m. we reached a point called Kirkharle, where the B6342 intersected with the A696, and there was ample space amongst the heaps of chippings to park for the night. I soon found a telephone box, phoned my niece, Mary, and described our position, which was 20 miles from Newcastle, and told her to bring a bottle of wine!

Megan prepared a lovely supper, and when Mary and her husband Stewart arrived, we settled down to discussing how best we could navigate through the city jungle of Newcastle, Gateshead and the outskirts of Sunderland. They all looked like one to me and we had no choice but to tackle the problem in the middle of the day. The alternative was to lose a day and I wasn't prepared to do that. Without revealing too much of her plans, Mary promised she would help by assisting with her car while Megan drove on with our car and caravan. After a couple of glasses (in reality it was cups!) of wine I stopped worrying and, before Mary left, we made arrangements that we would all meet in Newcastle airport car park which was four miles this side of the city, at 11 a.m.

Tuesday 12 July looked like being a lovely, warm, settled and sunny day. We were now clear of the hills and the mountains and back in the very rich farm lands of the Border Counties. We stopped for breakfast just beyond the village of Belsay and without too much difficulty we timed our arrival at the airport for 11 a.m. Megan was waiting in a lay-by very close to the entrance, which was fortunate as the car park itself is huge. We hadn't been parked more than five minutes when there was a tap on the door and a tall, middle-aged man introduced himself as Rod Griffiths of Tyne-Tees Television. This was obviously one of Mary's surprises and I began to wonder whatever else she might have in store for us.

12

The East Coast and the Fens to Lowestoft

It was very interesting to be part of a television programme and to see how the behind the scenes operations were executed. The three-minute story on the Tyne-Tees local evening news took well over an hour to organise. We drove off from the airport to find a quiet country road where the filming could take place in safety. After a few practice runs, the interviewer and myself jogged along behind a Ford Cortina estate with the 16-stone cameraman balanced precariously in the open boot. We were trying to keep a fairly precise distance of about ten feet between us and the car, and I kept worrying that the cameraman would suddenly fall out if the driver accelerated too much! As this nerve racking jog was taking place, the interviewer was firing rapid questions at me, which didn't somehow sound very natural. After completing this little run, Rod Griffiths and myself returned to where we had originally started from and ran the 200 yards back to the cameraman, who was crouched in the hedge, and presumably using a long distance lens!

I was embarrassingly breathless after this little sprint. Rod Griffiths was older than me and I discovered that he was training for the New York Marathon, so perhaps he was testing me!

When we returned to the caravan my niece, Mary, had arrived and she was very worried because she had organised a group of university runners to meet me in the middle of Newcastle at 1 p.m. We were six miles from the centre and it was after 12.30 p.m. so we had a problem. After a quick discussion we decided it was too important to miss the opportunity of being escorted through Newcastle and Gateshead, so all three of us, after saying cheerio to the TV crew, jumped into Mary's car and raced to the arranged meeting point in Newcastle.

I think there were about ten runners lined up in the car park when we arrived, and it was almost striking 1 p.m. Before I could catch my breath we were off, jogging through the busy streets of Newcastle with a very jolly bunch of students and, being local, they were completely familiar with their bearings as we ran through side streets, down narrow alleyways and across parks. Without any doubt, Megan and I would have lost each other in this jungle of roads. Eventually we surfaced from this maze of roads and crossed over the Tyne Bridge into Gateshead where Megan, Mary and Stewart met us. After taking a few photographs and thanking the students for guiding me safely through the city of Newcastle, Stewart gave me directions towards the A1, which would later connect with the A19 at a large roundabout. So, with no more than a five-minute break, I was running through the busy roads of Gateshead in search of this main southerly road to Middlesbrough with Mary promising to follow in about 20 minutes.

It was now nearly 2 p.m. and I was beginning to feel hungry and thirsty. After running for about four miles the heat of the sun was beginning to tire me and I was pouring with sweat, but no sign of Megan and Mary. I'd been watching the traffic carefully and I felt certain they hadn't raced past me. It was approximately 3 o'clock when I spotted the A1–A19 roundabout at Bolden Colliery and, to my delight, Mary and Megan finally arrived. As they slowed down I asked Mary to call in at a petrol station just ahead of us and buy a litre of lemonade whilst I completed a circuit of the roundabout.

Mary's busy day hadn't ended yet! She now had to drive back through Gateshead, Newcastle and drop me off at the airport. I still had that six-mile gap to fill that I'd missed out in the morning, and at 6 p.m. I had a dental appointment to collect my new plate!

I confess I was feeling very tired when I started that last session and asked Mary to keep in contact in case I had problems. About half way along the final leg, when I was nearly giving up, the girls had parked by a corner shop, so I stopped for a short break to enjoy an ice cream and a bar of chocolate. I had no idea where I was, but was blindly following Mary hoping she wouldn't get too far ahead. I had, however, forgotten to inform her that pedestrians are not allowed on motorways!

I was too tired to be concerned when I saw the motorway signs ahead and Mary's car disappearing down the link road. If I hadn't followed her I wouldn't have known where to go anyway! Actually,

15 Planning the route south with Mary's neighbour.

it was only a short strip about a mile long and, of course, motorways are particularly safe roads because of their very wide hard shoulders. I did see one police car, but they didn't appear to be interested in a lone runner.

It must have been about 5 o'clock when I staggered into the car-park to complete that six-mile missing gap. Mary raced back to her home in Gateshead so I could fall into a bath, change my clothes and another dash to the dentist back in Newcastle. By 6.30 we were back again in Gateshead, sitting in front of the TV waiting for the local news. With all the rushing around, and my new dental plate, I felt quite dizzy. I was beginning to understand the expression, 'I didn't know whether I was coming or going'!

I was not going to be spared. Philip David was suddenly appearing on Tyne-Tees TV. It was interesting, amusing and embarrassing, but I was pleased for Mary's sake. It was much better than I thought it would be so I assume a lot of editing took place. Although the day's run was only 26 miles, I was suffering more from nervous exhaustion than anything else.

We also had two visits from the local Press. This could have helped the cancer charity a great deal but sadly none of the charity people were present.

Friday 15 July was not an early start and, after breakfast, Mary escorted us back to the Bolden Colliery roundabout. My eldest brother was due to arrive at Mary's later that evening from Chester, so Megan and I agreed to drive back to Newcastle for a late family supper after completing our day's run.

During the morning several cars and lorries tooted their horns and I supposed it was because they had seen me on the previous evening's local TV news. It set me wondering how many puzzled motorists had seen me running out of the city in the afternoon and running back in again, from the airport direction, about two hours later!

I was not very impressed with the A19 dual carriageway as it had no hard shoulder to protect me from speeding traffic and the grass verge had an uneven surface, broken bottles and other rubbish. Furthermore, the grass and the thistles were uncut and it was difficult to decide which was the more dangerous, the grass verge or the traffic. It wasn't a very interesting route and I was quite pleased when we diverted from it at about 5 p.m. to take a quieter road (A1185) which passed the oil terminal before bringing us to the outskirts of Middlesbrough, where we crossed the Tees on the famous transporter bridge.

The city was fairly quiet and we had no difficulty in keeping in touch with one another as we negotiated our way through the centre and eventually to Stainton on the A174. I think we had added a few unnecessary miles, but at least we hadn't lost one another.

I kept going for another four miles—which was all built up area—until I caught up with Megan near a health centre in Ormesby. I didn't think the centre would object to us parking there overnight, even though they were displaying a 'Strictly No Parking' sign. It was now 7 p.m. and we would be leaving the following morning at about 6 a.m. So, I drove the car in, parked underneath the sign and, before unhitching the caravan, displayed our 'I am running for Cancer Relief' sign!

It took us an hour to drive back to Mary's house in Gateshead where I had another hot bath and we all enjoyed an excellent supper with the appropriate liquid refreshments. It was midnight before we took our leave and thanked Mary and Stewart for their kindness and hospitality. It was one of the highlights of our journey, but it was 1

16 On the run near Middlesbrough.

a.m. when we got back to our caravan in Ormesby.

Next morning I was an hour later than intended before I stumbled onto the road, with my eyes half-closed, my body not very willing to cooperate and a long, steep hill ahead of me! Unfortunately, we had a target of approximately 112 miles to complete to arrive in Grimsby on Monday evening at 5 p.m. It was only an average of 37 miles a day, which should not have presented too many difficulties. We had made arrangements to stay with friends, John and Margaret Richards, whom we had known for many years. John and I had sailed together on the west coast of Africa. I was second mate and he was third mate. He was now a lecturer at a local technical college.

We had no milk, so I had to wait for breakfast until Megan found a corner shop open in Guisborough, and then we stopped on the outskirts of the town. After the meal I was feeling a little more energetic, which was very fortunate as we were now climbing steeply onto the North York Moors. Luckily, it was a pleasant, warm but cloudy day with many touring buses struggling up the hills to enjoy the views and the heath lands of this National Park. Once we were on the top I thoroughly enjoyed the run and the views.

By late afternoon I started to descend from the moors to the plains and had a wonderful view of the port of Whitby and the North Sea. Sadly, I didn't run into the port itself as our route turned off just on the outskirts of the town, but very soon I was running uphill, yet again, towards Fylingdales Moor. Looking backwards and downwards, from the height of the moor, there was a magnificent view of the ruins of Whitby Abbey. This fine abbey stands on the east cliff and was founded by St Hilda in 657. Captain Cook, one of our greatest navigators, was born in the village of Marton, just south of Middlesbrough and about 25 miles from Whitby. For some years we lived close to Kaiti Hill, the point near Gisborne where Captain Cook first landed when he discovered New Zealand in October 1769. Coincidentally, my elder brother, Andrew, is a leading world expert on Captain Cook and his voyages of discovery.

It was a peaceful run across this moor and, when we had chalked up a total of 37 miles, Megan drove the car and caravan off the road and onto the heath land. It was a windy and exposed spot but we had very little choice apart from forest lands just ahead of us which I suspected might harbour midges and mosquitoes.

Soon after supper it poured with rain, but by this time we were cosily tucked up in bed working out tomorrow's route.

Sunday 15 July and the overnight rain was continuing. By 6.30 a.m. I decided I would just have to be brave, get wet, and get on with the job. I wasn't particularly brave, I did get wet and I did make some progress. We took an early breakfast, soon after passing through Cloughton, and it gave me the opportunity of changing my wet clothing.

The rain continued as we passed through the western suburbs of Scarborough. It was a typically wet and depressing Sunday morning with the streets almost deserted, except for the odd person scurrying through the rain for a newspaper. I was able to take a short cut to a village called Seamer, which saved about a mile, while Megan had to go the slightly longer way round.

By mid morning the rain had stopped, the sun came out, and in 20 minutes I felt completely dry and was able to discard my showerproof clothing when I caught up with Megan. We were near Staxton and Megan was looking a little worried. She had parked on a gentle slope, got into the caravan and was in the process of peeling some potatoes for the evening meal, when she suddenly noticed the hedge was moving! It took a few seconds before she realised the hedge was securely anchored but car and caravan were gathering speed with no one at the controls! I understand she managed an excellent sprint from the caravan to the car and she hasn't forgotten that handbrakes exist!

We took the B1249 road, climbed for about a mile into the Yorkshire Wolds and were heading almost due south on a straight course for the Humber Bridge, which was still nearly 36 miles away. It was a very peaceful run, with the sun shining and hardly any traffic. At one point I was cruising along the grass verge, enjoying the beautiful view of open countryside and golden corn as far as the eye could see, when I nearly stepped on a covey of young partridges. I don't know which of us had the biggest fright as they suddenly whirred up in front of me, popped over the hedge and flew fast and low across the cornfield.

We lunched near Langtoft, by-passed Great Driffield, and reached Beverley at about 6 p.m. We found an excellent camping site three miles south of the town and about seven miles from the Humber Bridge. Apart from the wet morning it had been easy running and I was pleased with a score of 44 miles.

On Monday morning we had an extra hour's sleep as we had previously arranged to cross the bridge at 11 a.m., which also gave Megan an opportunity to replenish our fruit and groceries in Willersby, a suburb of Hull. It was another fine day but, for no particular reason, I felt very tired and I found it necessary to stop running and walk for quite long periods.

I crossed this two-mile bridge on time and met Megan for the mid morning break about another mile further on. Like the Severn and Forth bridges, the Humber Bridge is a massive construction, but from either approach it looks very elegant. I was surprised to read, in the statistics, that it contains 16,500 tonnes of steel and nearly the same weight in cables (11,000 tonnes)!

During coffee, John Richard's son Jonathan arrived from Grimsby on his bicycle and, later on, at lunch time, John also called in en route from Hull to Grimsby to collect his bike.

By 3 p.m. I was flanked by two cyclists and exhausting myself trying to keep up a reasonable pace. As I explained earlier, it wasn't my most energetic day.

John had made arrangements for me to meet the Press, so once again we abandoned the run, drove into Grimsby for the interview and, an hour later, drove back out to the parked caravan to complete the journey properly and on foot.

I was very tired by the time we reached John's home and I felt this was due, in part, to various pressures and pushing myself too much to keep in touch with my escorts. Anyway, I was soon revived after a two-foot deep hot bath and an ice cold shandy.

After supper I was interviewed by Mrs Christine Dunn, the first member of the Macmillan Cancer Relief Fund that I had seen since leaving Wool!

To complete the day, Margaret provided an excellent evening meal and we retired quite early to bed. I had only run 32 miles for the day but my grand total was getting close to 2,000 miles.

It wasn't easy to make an early start on the Tuesday morning, which didn't surprise me! After breakfast I had to wait patiently by the telephone for a talk-back interview with Radio Humberside that John or Margaret had organised. Actually, when the call came, I quite enjoyed it and I wasn't as nervous as I thought I might be. It was a sensible conversation, discussing various aspects of our journey around Britain and, hopefully, it helped the cancer charity. The call ended with the interviewer informing his listeners that I was leaving Grimsby within the hour, running down the A16 towards Louth, and wearing the green Macmillan Cancer Relief singlet.

Immediately after this interview Jonathan drove us to the town hall where we met the town clerk who insisted we should all celebrate the occasion with a glass of sherry! We sped back to the house, where I changed into my running gear, and managed to be jogging out of Grimsby within the hour. Megan went ahead with car and caravan, piloted by Jonathan, and John was escorting me on his bicycle. We all met up about five miles south of the city, where we had a break for coffee before saying cheerio to our friends as they returned to Grimsby and we carried on through the Lincolnshire countryside towards Louth and Boston.

During the morning a few motorists, who obviously recognised who I was, tooted and waved as they passed. I must admit I did enjoy this bit of publicity and it was quite a boost for my morale.

The tow-bar was causing Megan some concern. It looked as though the hydraulic system had broken down which posed difficulties when stopping or starting, towing on hills and particularly when driving in traffic. Megan stopped at two large caravan centres where one of them had the part but wasn't prepared to mend it until the next day, and the next garage hadn't got the part anyway. Megan was told to try in King's Lynn, which was still a couple of days ahead of us. Fortunately it looked as though there were no steep hills immediately ahead of us to negotiate.

It was a warm, humid day and I still didn't feel at all energetic. We passed through Louth soon after lunch and, during the afternoon and evening, I ran through a succession of small villages until we finally camped on the outskirts of the town of Spilsby. We only just managed 30 miles for the day.

On Wednesday 18 July I was off to an early start at 6 a.m. but I had a worrying injury problem—a pain in my left leg, just behind my ankle. I decided not to take any risks, so for most of the day I walked, but I felt quite pleased to reach our 2,000-mile mark as I gently jogged through Boston after 60 days. Coming from Wales and the West Country, we were not used to mile after mile of flat, open country. As well as the corn crops there were acres and acres of vegetables such as cabbages, cauliflowers, carrots, potatoes and peas. We were now in the Fens and our route was taking us south of The Wash at an average distance of about four miles from the sea. The land was very flat, with hardly any hedgerows, but quite a lot of wild roses growing wherever they could find an opportunity. I found it a little boring, and very frustrating, not being able to run properly.

By mid afternoon I walked through Fosdyke, followed by Saracen's Head and finally camping near Gedney. Before supper we went for a drive in search of a shandy and a telephone box. We found both and also visited the parish church of Gedney. This beautiful marshland church contains a fourteenth-century brass and a number of alabaster effigies. Gedney itself had been threatened by flooding, not only from the sea but also from fresh water brought down by rivers into the fen. Fen breaks have been built to the south-west and sea banks to the north-east.

Thursday 19 July was a cold and overcast morning, but my leg was fully recovered and I was jogging along soon after 6 a.m. The countryside was dead flat for miles around and it was the largest market garden I had ever seen anywhere. We stopped for breakfast after crossing the Nene at Sutton Bridge. It was late morning when I ran across the Ouse and entered the attractive town of King's Lynn.

The town has a long history, and its medieval buildings are some of the finest in the country. We tried, but failed, to get the caravan tow-bar repaired, but at least we were able to purchase the necessary part. We left the town on the B1145 road, hoping it would be a little quieter and more interesting than the main road to Norwich.

We were now entering Norfolk and the scenery was changing rapidly with hedgerows along the road. The countryside was undulating with small woodlands and some pasture. In the main, we were back to the corn crops and gradually leaving the market gardening behind us.

By teatime we were in the depths of the country and it was a beautiful English summer's afternoon with the larks singing their beaks off! Running along this quiet roadside the grass verges were red with the gentle, swinging corn poppies and the mauve scabious. It was a beautiful sight against acre upon acre of ripening wheat and barley crops. The abundance of the harvest was almost unbelievable and stretched as far as the eye could see in every direction. We hadn't seen any evidence of any poor crops of any sort on the whole east coast, from the Border counties 400 miles further north to the Fens.

Running through the countryside I had little else to do other than witness my immediate surroundings and environment and to think about what I had observed. Amid this beauty I could imagine some sadness. The poppies brought to mind stories my father used to tell us of the battlefields of Flanders and, as for the harvests, I wondered how much would be distributed to the starving people of the Third World. There appeared something too perfect about these crops—there were hardly any weeds—and as a result probably fewer birds and fewer wild flowers. I wondered how much thought the farmers had given to the environment before they ripped out hundreds of miles of hedgerows and whether they appreciated that, as owners of that land, they were also custodians of that heritage for our future generations.

Although we all grumble about our British climate, it is the wonder of the changing seasons that enables us to appreciate this delightful poem that we all sang as children. No wonder it's so popular, and generally so appropriate, as a harvest festival hymn.

> We plough the fields, and scatter
> The Good Seed on the land,
> But it is fed and watered,
> By God's Almighty hand;

He sends the snow in winter,
The warmth to swell the grain,
The breezes and the sunshine,
And soft, refreshing rain.
He only is the maker
Of all things near and far,
He paints the wayside flower,
He lights the evening star.
The winds and waves obey Him,
By Him the birds are fed;
Much more to us, His children,
He gives our daily bread.

I had been very fortunate to spend nearly the whole summer running through this countryside of Britain, seeing so much of its beauty, which is bound to leave a lasting impression on me. It's quite different from driving through it, when everything passes so quickly, and you are closed in a machine where you can neither feel or smell the land.

All through the afternoon and evening we continued to progress slowly along this B road. It was easy to relax as there was hardly any traffic and the weather was cool and cloudy, with only a light breeze.

We camped in a wide field entrance at 7 p.m., having run 39 miles, and very soon after supper it started to rain quite heavily.

As we set off early on Friday morning it was drizzling and cold and I had noticed the petrol gauge at nought when resetting the mileometer. I told Megan to drive ahead of me and not wait behind, in case she ran out of fuel, as I didn't expect to find any petrol stations open until 8.

We breakfasted at Bawdeswell, just after joining the A1067, and also refuelled. Megan went on ahead of me to see if she could find a garage on the outskirts of Norwich capable of fixing the German gas-filled damper tow-bar connection.

After breakfast I set off in clean, dry clothing and wearing my showerproof coat and trousers. At about 11 a.m. I ran into Taverham, which is really a suburb of Norwich, and Megan was waiting for me by a paper shop. She had found a small garage who were prepared to do the necessary repairs, so I followed her up the side street where I found this one-man outfit attacking the towing mechanism of our caravan. It looked as though most of the nuts and bolts were seized

17 Merlin in the wayside poppies and barley of Norfolk.

up with a decade of rust! It was Friday, and I had visions of us being stranded here until Monday. This one-man band had effected the repairs, assembled the new damper and completed the job in one hour. He only charged us £10 and the damper itself had cost £19. A garage near King's Lynn had quoted us £90 to supply and fit the part if we had come back the following day! So, we had just saved ourselves £61 and, furthermore, it was a job well done that had been worrying Megan for several days. Unfortunately, I lost an hour's running time but, nevertheless, we decided to get clear of Norwich before stopping for lunch. We were disappointed at not being able to spare time to visit this city with its cathedral dating from Norman times.

My route took me clear of the city centre by means of a circular road which I eventually left to join the A146 en route for our final cardinal point at Lowestoft. Megan was waiting for me at this point, so I stopped for a late lunch. After lunch I ran for another eight miles before stopping for tea just beyond the pretty market town of Loddon, which has retained an olde worlde atmosphere. The little fifteenth-century church contains a painting of Sir James Hobart and his wife. Sir James was attorney general to Henry VII.

It was now another fine summer's evening, but not as warm as I would have liked. The last stretch took us through a few more small villages before arriving at Beccles, the most southerly boating point of the Norfolk Broads. Beccles is situated on the river Waveney and its main claim to fame is its church where Nelson's parents were married. It also has a separate tower, 92 feet high, with some superb views over the surrounding marshes.

We actually camped about a mile beyond the town, adjacent to a roundabout, which had a spare triangular piece of land, so I drove the caravan onto this and hoped we wouldn't be moved on by the police. We were not disturbed. They probably thought we were gypsies, so left us alone!

It was dull and overcast on Saturday morning as I set off at 6 a.m. towards Lowestoft. It was only an eight-mile run, which I did very slowly, stopping for a cup of tea at a half-way point. We reached Lowestoft at 8 and headed straight for the sea, where we found an almost deserted car park right on the sea front.

This is Britain's most easterly town and, besides being a fishing port, it is also a popular holiday resort. It has rail links with Norwich and London and is only a stone's throw from the Broads. Although there is a plaque somewhere in Lowestoft, denoting the most easterly point, I didn't find it but assume I must have been close enough to it!

So now, after nearly 63 days and 2,100 miles, I had run to the most northerly, southerly, easterly and westerly points of the United Kingdom. All that now remained to be done was to complete the circuit at Wool, another 250 miles further on, but I felt it would be the most difficult and testing section of our journey. Up to now I had avoided giving serious thought as to how I was going to run through London, although I had made the decision to run through it and not round it. There should be a little more excitement ahead of us before the end of this venture!

13

The Final Leg through London

After breakfast we strolled along Lowestoft's sandy beach before departing from England's most easterly town, along the A12 towards London and the Home Counties. We had left the more sparsely populated rural areas of East Anglia and the Fens and had arrived in the more densely populated south-easterly corner of the kingdom.

The A12 is the arterial road joining London with Chelmsford, Colchester, Ipswich and Lowestoft, with link roads to Harwich from Colchester and to Felixstowe (Britain's largest container port) from Ipswich. Obviously, from now on the road would become busier and busier and probably more hazardous for a runner. Today being a Saturday, we were spared juggernauts and the ordinary holiday traffic was friendly and posed no problems.

The landscape was changing, with less arable land and more green pastures and woodlands. There were still vast acreages of ripening wheat and barley plus a fair share of sugar beet and other vegetable crops. As the day progressed it became more and more humid, but I felt quite strong and had completed nearly 20 miles when we stopped for lunch, which was after crossing the river Blyth and emerging the other side of Blythburgh.

Megan's Aunt Nan lived in Kelsale and we had been invited for supper at 7 p.m., so I planned to run as far as I could, when we would mark our spot, and return to Kelsale to camp, dine and, hopefully, bath! At 3 I passed Megan parked in Kelsale near a telephone box, presumably reporting our progress and our estimated time of arrival for the evening meal. I suspect Aunt Nan's invitations are not to be treated casually! If dinner is to be served at 7 there would be frowns if we were late!

It was a very warm afternoon and I was drinking copious amounts of lemonade and orange squash. At one point I was attacked by thousands of little black midges but, fortunately, it was either a passing army or they were at a permanent site and I was just passing through! Soon after this encounter a wasp or a bee flew into my open mouth and I very nearly swallowed it. I was lucky it didn't sting me.

Saxmundham, Stratford St Andrew and Marlesford were all pretty Suffolk villages that I ran through during the late afternoon and evening. I finally stopped beyond Marlesford at a turning to Campsey Ash. I joined Megan at this point, where we turned the car and caravan around and returned to the village of Kelsale where we found Aunt Nan's home and a space to park the caravan. There was just sufficient time for me to have a quick bath before 7 p.m. dinner, but I suspect I missed out on a glass of sherry! Once again, it was a great thrill to relax in space, and armchairs, and enjoy a roast meal.

After supper we talked until quite late, but slept in the caravan, which we had parked in the yard. We thanked Aunt Nan for her kindness and excellent hospitality before retiring to bed as we anticipated driving out quietly at the crack of dawn.

I was now carefully trying to plan the final phase of this journey. I calculated that we could possibly complete the distance in another six days, which would mean arriving in Wool on Friday 27 July. That would give us the opportunity of spending the weekend with our daughters in Taunton and to relax for 48 hours before returning to work on the following Monday morning. I fell asleep estimating that the distance remaining was over 200 miles, but less than 250, so I would need to average 40 miles per day.

There were two main problems:

1 At this very late stage I still hadn't resolved how to tackle

    a physically running through London
    b how Megan was going to negotiate the same problem, towing the caravan
    c communication between the two of us during this critical period.

2 I was at a peak of fitness but any slight injury problem could still arise, and I knew I would feel bitterly disappointed if it became necessary to abandon the adventure when success was so near at hand. Mentally I was beginning to tire, perhaps it was the continual strain after 60 days of waking early each morning and facing a forty-mile run. At times my concentration

was not as well disciplined as it was a few weeks ago. I would need to sharpen this considerably by Monday morning when I estimated running into a volume of traffic that would be greater than any we had experienced so far.

Sunday morning at 5.30 we drove very quietly out of Aunt Nan's gates and headed for last night's finishing point a little beyond Marlesford. It was a fine but muggy day and already warm as I began the day's run by walking up a fairly steep hill at the start of a dual carriageway system which by-passed Wickham Market, before levelling off into undulating countryside. After five miles of walking and jogging slowly, I stopped for breakfast in a lay-by close to Woodbridge. This former port at the mouth of the river Deben is now a popular sailing centre. Attractive houses of major historical interest surround the old market square, many dating from the sixteenth to the nineteenth centuries with picturesque Dutch gables.

Soon after running through Martlesham I came across some complicated signs and traffic lights and decided to wait for Megan in case we took different routes. Often she would stay behind me to wash up, clean the caravan or take the dog for a walk. This caused delays when I came across these unexpected situations, when I had no map to consult, and all I could do was sit on the roadside and wait. The intersection turned out to be a new link road to Felixstowe from the north of Ipswich which had only recently been opened. This was close to the approaches to Ipswich and I decided, as it was a Sunday, that I would run through the centre of the city and agreed to meet Megan back on the A12 dual carriageway at the first lay-by near Capel St Mary. I guessed that we wouldn't meet again for about ten miles, so I took two glasses of lemonade before heading for Ipswich, which I found to be surprisingly busy for a Sunday. I got lost in the centre and, by the time I got my correct bearings, must have added an extra couple of miles.

It appeared to be a beautiful city and I saw several well preserved timber-framed houses. Megan navigated through the city with no apparent difficulties and was waiting, with lunch laid out, when I finally arrived a little late at our planned meeting point. As usual, I was more thirsty than hungry, but it was becoming a particularly warm day and the perspiration was running off me in rivers!

I was astonished at the build up of traffic since reaching Ipswich, and I could only guess what it would be like tomorrow as we got closer to London. With the caravan swaying with the 'zip, zip' of passing traffic, this hardly seemed like John Constable country with its rolling meadows, rustic villages and where life moves at an easy pace. The cars were speeding past at 70–80 mph and I could hardly wait for tomorrow's juggernauts!

During the afternoon the shin splint problem recurred and I had to slow down by alternatively jogging for a couple of miles and then walking the same distance. It was very hot weather, the traffic was getting worse, and my leg felt very painful. There was no hard shoulder, just a 9-inch wide paving stone to run on. Later this reduced to about 6 inches. My leg not only felt painful but actually looked swollen. I kept rubbing it with Deep Heat, hoping it might do some good. I had already committed myself to an appointment with the cancer charity headquarters in Dorset Square at 10 a.m. on Tuesday, and I intended being there on time.

By 7 a.m. I had jogged, walked and limped as far as a point called Feering, having passed a couple of miles to the west of Colchester. At Feering we left the A12, just to get a break from the constant traffic, then stopped at Kelvedon where we bought a fish and chip supper. After a rest and some telephone calls I decided we should add a few more miles before camping. It was rare to run after supper, but I was becoming very agitated and concerned as to how we would possibly deal with the daytime traffic on this busy road.

After running for about two miles the B road rejoined the A12 and it was already dark. I told Megan to drive down the dual carriageway and take the first turning off to the left, which looked about a mile away. It was quite irresponsible of me to run in the dark on such a road and I make no excuses for my folly. It was only a mile, and as soon as Megan turned off the main road she parked in the Rivenhall Motor Inn car park. I sought out the proprietor who very kindly allowed us to remain there for the night. So we settled down to enjoy a couple of shandies in comfort before retiring to the caravan. I was happy about the day's total of 43 miles, but concerned about the shin splints.

Monday 23 July was likely to be our most difficult day and I had been restless for most of the night, hearing a nearby clock chime most of the hours. At 4.30 a.m. I got up, had my glass of milk and plate of cornflakes, and was pounding down the dual carriageway by 5. To my astonishment, the shin splint problem had completely disappeared! By 6 the juggernauts were out in force and thundering past in convoys travelling at the speed of sound. It was like a conveyor belt and the constant noise of the traffic began to fray my nerves. At 8 I ran into the centre of Chelmsford and even at this early hour there was a huge traffic jam stretching right through the town. I caught up with Megan, who was boxed in by traffic at a bus stop, and I decided to break for breakfast, or until the police moved us on.

By 9 a.m. I was back on the road again and it was already a very hot day. Soon after clearing Chelmsford we were on a one-way, three-lane road. With all the heavy vehicles, noise and heat, it felt dangerous, but in reality there was quite a wide, well-marked hard shoulder to run on. On the other hand, I didn't expect to ever meet any early morning joggers on this road and I can remember one frightening experience when I had to run across what felt like no man's land where another three-lane section came in from my left. To the three lanes of traffic speeding past on my right, and the other three lanes on my left, I must have looked like a frightened rabbit trying to escape the madness! As for myself, I could see the funny side of the 30-second dash 'over the top' and I felt particularly lonely and vulnerable—like a canoeist in a rapid without his paddle!

At noon relief was at hand as I turned off this speedway and headed for the town centre of Brentwood. Megan was parked on yellow lines near the town centre and it gave me the chance to quench my thirst and make arrangements to meet her for lunch another three miles along the B186. Megan said she would wait while I went off to the bank to draw some money, but when I came back she had obviously been told to move on. So I set off on the B186 towards the Dartford Tunnel carrying £200 in my hand!

I soon realised that one of the direction signs was half hidden by an overhanging tree and guessed that Megan had probably gone the wrong way. After a couple of miles I telephoned the police who very kindly set off to look for her. When they located Megan they unfortunately told her that I was in the Warley Hospital, instead of saying I was phoning from a box *outside* the hospital. They escorted Megan back to my position and, after thanking them for their help, we set off again on our journey, having unfortunately lost nearly an hour. We, therefore, had a very quick lunch as we hoped to avoid the rush-hour traffic at the Dartford Tunnel.

It was a surprisingly peaceful and quiet run along the B186 and, for the first time, we saw wheat that had ripened sufficiently for harvesting. It was just after 4 p.m. when I ran through South

Ockendon and I continued for about another mile before meeting up with Megan again. We were now nearly three miles from the tunnel and we decided it was too risky for me to attempt to run any closer in case Megan couldn't park anywhere to wait for me. So I gave up the running and we set off together towards the Dartford Tunnel with the intention of dropping me off at the first roundabout on the other side of the Thames. When we reached the other side there was so much traffic and so many road junctions that Megan persuaded me not to stop. We made another quick decision to continue right into London, find a spot to park the caravan for the night, have tea, and then drive back later in the evening, without the caravan, to complete this last section.

We passed through Dartford, linked up with the A2, located the South Circular Road, and finally turned south on the A24, signed for Worthing. We were now in Clapham and desperately looking for any spot where we could park the caravan. After turning down several side streets we eventually found a spare space in Foxbourne Road, off Ritherdon Road. It had taken us longer than I had thought and so, after a quick tea and cake, and Megan had filled the thermos, we collected a litre of lemonade, disconnected the caravan and set off back to the southern side of the Dartford Tunnel.

It was 8 p.m. when I stepped out of the car to attempt this final section. I had run 30 miles up to the tunnel and I intended finishing the other section, even if it was midnight. It was a very warm evening with heavy, overcast thunder clouds rumbling around. I didn't enjoy the dual carriageway stretch of the A2 as I felt boxed in, and the oppressive weather didn't help. It was getting dark when I reached the South Circular Road, and for the most part I was able to run on pavements. Megan kept me well supplied with lemonade and chocolate and, without the caravan, it was fairly easy for her to keep me in sight. I ran through one or two 'dodgy' areas with poor street lighting, but I didn't think anyone would be interested in mugging a lone runner. In any case, by this time I was no longer carrying the £200! It was striking 11 p.m. as I turned down the A24 with just over a mile to run and, apart from a few drunks, the streets were almost deserted. I was very tired, but surprised I had managed to run the 19 miles in just over three hours, particularly as I had already run 30 miles earlier in the day. I would have to settle for 49 miles as my best day's run—I never did run a 50-miler.

Tuesday morning was another warm, overcast day and, after an early breakfast, we caught the tube to Marylebone Station where we met my niece, Elizabeth, and also Philippa, who was secretary to the Macmillan Cancer Relief Fund. Philippa then escorted me to the charity's headquarters in Dorset Square where we met Major Garnett, their chairman, and various other members of the staff. After coffee and cakes, photographers from *The Times* and Thames TV arrived and I had to change into my running gear and suffer a half hour photographic session running up and down a side street adjacent to Dorset Square. Hopefully, all in a good cause! We took our leave, after a final group photograph, with Elizabeth determined to drive us back to our caravan, through central London in the lunchtime rush hour. It isn't that I think my niece is a bad driver, or a poor navigator, but it was an interesting experience to note that the traffic lights, whether on red or green, did not interfere with her progress. She seemed quite at home driving in the right hand lane, continental fashion, in the middle or, conservatively, on the traditional left hand side. Her navigation was simple and straightforward—an A–Z on her lap, which she read at her convenience and to the consternation of other road users! On the credit side, we saw Trafalgar Square twice and Piccadilly Circus three times! Nevertheless, the exciting one-hour jaunt brought us safely back to the caravan, where we steadied ourselves with a glass of wine! It had been great fun seeing Elizabeth again, and she had been such a valuable communications link with the rest of the family during our journey around the country. After Elizabeth departed we had a quick lunch, connected the caravan and drove off down the A24 towards Worthing.

Megan drove and I studied the route carefully as we passed through Epsom, Leatherhead and Dorking. After Dorking we started to look for a suitable camping site, which we finally found on a side road at Beare Green. Once again, it was a quick cup of tea, disconnect the caravan and race back into London so I could start my day's run from Foxbourne Road. Unfortunately, we ran into the evening rush hour traffic coming out of London so I didn't actually start the day's run until 4.30 p.m. and this time I knew the distance was 23 miles. It was a surprisingly safe passage. I enjoyed running on the crowded pavements and managed to keep a fairly steady pace despite the crowds. I did feel tired and stiff from the previous evening's late night run, and I had to stop at a chemist shop to buy a tube of Deep Heat to rub on my hip.

Megan and I met quite often, which I found reassuring, because I

18 The sprint finish at Wool.

was physically and mentally quite exhausted from the various activities of the last 48 hours. The weather too was very humid which made me perspire a great deal and I needed drinks regularly. By the time I reached Dorking it was nearly dusk and I was walking more than I was running. I was very pleased to reach that caravan and thankful it wasn't even 100 yards further on, but it was surprising how quickly I revived after a shandy!

Wednesday morning we woke at 3 a.m. with thunder, lightening and heavy rain rattling on the roof of the caravan. I managed to sleep, on and off, for the next couple of hours, but was on the road soon after 6 and almost immediately we left the A24, heading for Billingshurst on the A29, with dry roads but an overcast sky. At 7 a.m. it started to pour with rain and it became much cooler. I kept going for another hour until I was almost waterlogged!

At breakfast I floated out of my wet clothing, rubbed myself down and sat down to breakfast with the blood successfully circulating again! I had now set my sights on completing this ordeal at noon on Friday at Wool. I calculated that I would need to run 110 miles in the next 2½ days, which meant that I wouldn't have time to dawdle!

It was still raining heavily when I restarted after breakfast, and my hip, although better, was still a little stiff, but I felt that with a bit of luck everything should hold together for another 2½ days.

I was too wet and uncomfortable to stop for mid morning coffee and didn't see much of Billingshurst as I trotted through with the rain pouring off the end of my nose! At 12 o'clock the rain had ceased and, when I caught up with Megan, I changed all my clothes again and enjoyed a hot Bovril. While I was resting, Chris Scarron, photographer for the 'Couples' feature in the *Mail on Sunday*, arrived and spent an hour taking photographs of us. I'd phoned him on the previous evening and told him our route and wondered if we would see him. He didn't delay us very much. All I lost was about half an hour of my rest period.

It remained dull and overcast for the rest of the day but, fortunately, there was no more rain. During the afternoon I ran through beautiful Sussex countryside passing through Petworth, close to Cowdray Park, across the river Rother at Midhurst, with the rolling downs to the south of us. It was late evening when I crossed the Rother again, prior to running through the Hampshire town of Petersfield. We continued on the A272 for another couple of miles until Megan found an excellent parking spot, just 50 yards off the main road, on the little village green at Langrish. We were parked alongside the telephone box!

Considering the very wet morning I was quite satisfied with the day's score of 41 miles, but I would still need a big effort tomorrow. I estimated 69 miles to go, in 1½ days.

Thursday 26 July dawned a lovely, sunny day and I was off to a very early 5 a.m. start. My hip continued to be painful but certainly wasn't getting any worse and, in general, I was feeling a little stiff.

19 Commander Nash and his team welcoming us back at Wool.

On balance, I was very fit and had to accept a few aches and pains, but today I appreciated that I still needed one last big effort to place me in a good position to complete the course by noon tomorrow. The early morning run was quiet and relaxing and I noticed that not only was the wheat ripe in this area but some had already been harvested. The hedges were full of hazelnuts and there was an abundance of beech mast in the woodlands.

About two miles east of Winchester I joined the A33 dual carriage-way and somewhere near Twyford I had to negotiate a particularly dangerous couple of miles. It was one of those situations where there was no hard shoulder at all, just a metal barrier at the edge of the road, with very busy, heavy and fast traffic heading south for Southampton. Fortunately, this didn't last more than about three miles when I was able to link on to the A31 and head for Romsey.

I caught up with Megan at a small village called Ampfield and we sat out in the sun to enjoy our lunch, but I didn't have my usual after lunch rest. At 2.30 I had reached Romsey, a market town which is not strikingly attractive, apart from an abbey. On the southern outskirts lies Broadlands, home of the late Earl Mountbatten, and here I crossed the Test, famous for its trout fishing. A charming river, running through rich and pleasant country, but the fishing rights are the preserve of the wealthy few!

We were now heading south-west, towards Ringwood, on a dual carriageway through Stoney Cross and the northern section of the New Forest. It was a long, boring run but it was comforting to think that our mission was nearly complete. It had all been a tremendous thrill but I realised that I was slowly running out of steam.

Soon after 7 p.m. I ran through Ringwood, across the river Avon, and into Dorset. We found an ideal camping site in a picnic area about two miles beyond Ringwood, but I actually ran a further two miles where Megan came to collect me after disconnecting the caravan. I'd run 48 miles, leaving 22 to complete the journey tomorrow morning.

How fortunate we were that our last day should turn out to be warm, sunny and friendly! As I ran through those last 22 miles south of Ringwood back to Wool, through the outskirts of Bournemouth, I kept wondering whether or not it would be a dream! Three years ago I couldn't even run a mile and now I was about to complete an exciting and interesting 2,354-mile adventure that had taken me to the furthest corners of the kingdom. By my own standards, this was a personal best, and I felt delighted and excited to have nearly completed such an unlikely marathon journey. I wished I could share my feeling of joy with those friends who had helped and motivated me. To accomplish a run of this magnitude is not an impossible goal and it is well within the capabilities of every healthy, ordinary man or woman, from the age of 25 to 60+. To succeed, however, I believe there has to be mental determination in one form or another. The will to win, the fear of failure, a bet or, perhaps, simply a labour of love.

The human body has far greater powers of adaptability and endurance than most people give it credit for. I did the run with only two days' ill-health at the very beginning, without a day's rest, and without any special diet or food supplement of any kind. I was fitter at the end of the 70 days than when I started.

I have placed this paragraph in italics because the sentiments and facts are almost identical to those expressed by Bruce Tulloh in his book *Four Million Footsteps* when he ran across America from Los Angeles to New York in 1969. He didn't even experience two days' ill-health, and his time was five days shorter than mine. The first sentence needs underlining!

I shall be very fortunate to be left with a wonderful bonus — lasting memories from different parts of Britain's countryside. The Longships lighthouse at Land's End, Cardigan Bay, the storm clouds rolling up the valley in Glencoe, looking across the Pentland Firth to the Old Man of Hoy on the Orkneys, the golden waving corn harvest, the wayside wild flowers and the friendly sandpipers and oystercatchers — to name but a few. Or the sight of me scurrying down the A12, just north of London, like a scared rabbit, must have amused some of those juggernaut drivers!

I know I'm the one in the spotlight but I also know that I could not have achieved my goal without my wife's constant help, support and encouragement. I'm proud of Megan's courage and skill in towing our caravan for those two thousand odd miles without a scratch. Perhaps I sometimes think 'We did it my way', but we did not, 'We did it our way'! It was a team effort.

14

Learning from Others

Between 1973 and 1979 we lived in New Zealand. That was some years before I started on my running career!

Our youngest daughter, Sarah, had joined the local swimming club, and it wasn't very long before I was roped in as a timekeeper for their Monday night club races. Sarah was becoming a very good swimmer, and I soon became quite involved and took a great interest in her progress. On occasions Sarah and I worked together—outside the swimming club—but in the new Gisborne Olympic Pool, where she wanted to attempt some longer distances. It usually meant getting up very early on a Saturday or Sunday morning so we could have the pool almost to ourselves. At age 11 I timed Sarah over the 800 metres distance (16 lengths) at 17 minutes 2 seconds. I was so proud of her effort that I awarded her a 'Special Certificate of Merit'!

Two years later, at the age of 13, in March 1979, she swam her first mile. This involved 32.19 laps of the 50-metre pool. What I found so interesting was how well she paced herself over the distance: lap 2 was 49 seconds and lap 11 was 51 seconds. The eight laps in between were six at 51 seconds, one at 52 and one at 53. The pattern was much the same throughout the 32.19 laps. She actually completed the mile in 27 minutes 49 seconds at an average of 51.85 seconds per lap.

I learned a lot from not only watching Sarah, but other swimmers as well. Several years later, when I started running, I soon remembered how very important and energy saving it was to be able to flow at a steady and constant pace—almost like freewheeling. I did seriously learn a lot from my involvement with the swimming club and working with my teenage daughter. It's interesting how these little gems of knowledge surface years later when you really need them. As for my own swimming ability—well, I was completely hopeless!

15

Conclusions, Facts and Figures

Departed from Wool Post Office at noon, Friday 18 May 1984.

Arrived back at the same point at noon, Friday 27 July

Total time and distance = 70 days and 2,354 miles

Daily average distance = 33.63 miles

Or 89.8 marathons run in 70 days!

1.28 marathon distances per day!

For the major part of our journey we used the 3 miles to the inch Ordnance Survey *Motoring Atlas of Great Britain.* We used other maps in Scotland. I calculated the daily distances on the Ordnance Survey atlas with a precision pair of dividers. This was checked in conjunction with the 'reset' car mileometer, particularly in the built-up areas.

After completing this run, I submitted to the AA Home Routes Processing Unit, at Fanum House in Bristol, a detailed route of our course from start to finish. Their total distance was 2,414 miles, which was exactly 60 miles more than my figure. I prefer to use my own calculations, but I am very grateful to Mr MacDonald at the AA for his efforts which confirm that my figures are fair and reasonable. In no way are we involved in any records, so the figures I quote are sufficiently accurate for various comparisons and statistics.

If we divided the total time of 70 days into 4 quarterly stages of 17½ days, we get the following results:

1st 17½-day period I ran 455 miles. Daily average = 26.00

miles (near Newport, South Wales)

2nd 17½-day period I ran 545 miles. Daily average = 31.14 miles (Glasgow)

3rd 17½-day period I ran 689 miles. Daily average = 39.37 miles (Edinburgh)

4th 17½-day period I ran 665 miles. Daily average = 38.00 miles (Wool)

The first 35 days I ran 1,000 miles, averaging 28.57 miles (Glasgow)

The second 35 days I ran 1,354 miles, averaging 38.68 miles

The overall 70 days was 2,354 miles, averaging 33.63 miles

It can be seen that I actually averaged ten miles a day more in the second phase of the journey.

The only comparison I can make is with Bruce Tulloh's run across America in 1969. His total distance 2,876 miles, time taken 64 days 21 hours 50 minutes, daily average 44.31 miles per day, 11 miles a day more than mine! He was running across a more difficult terrain, with far greater extremes of climate. From a slimming point of view I was more successful, losing seven pounds to his six!

I did not become involved in any special diet but, for obvious reasons, I avoided heavy meals and greasy foods. As it was summer we ate a great deal of fruit and salad and there were naturally cooking restrictions with a caravan stove. So it was basically milk, cheese, eggs, fruit, biscuits, cake, cold meats and salad. Drinks included tea, lemonade, orange juice, Bovril, Ovaltine and shandy. I rarely drank water!

I started the run with three pairs of well-used shoes, 'New Balance', 'Silver Shadow' and 'Dunlop SA26'. When I reached Chester I was given a second pair of 'Silver Shadows' and also bought a third pair. From Chester I sent the 'Dunlop SA26' away to be resoled and heeled and I collected them at Newcastle. I changed my shoes regularly—at least five times a day—and the wear on the heels I built up with 'Shoe-Goo'. It seems to surprise a lot of people when I tell them that I still have all five pairs, in perfectly usable condition, two pairs being my original purchases.

In order to avoid injuries and health problems, I believe it is particularly important for middle-aged men and women who are contemplating taking up jogging or running to do so with a carefully planned training schedule. There is a tremendous amount of excellent advice to be found in the various running and marathon magazines and they all stress the importance of a gradual build-up to fitness. Once you have reached a reasonable level of fitness I see no dangers in pushing yourself when you merely feel tired, but alternatively it is imperative you stop and rest if you have unusual pains or feel unwell. These are surely warning signals to take it easy. In the old days, when we purchased a new car, it had a 'running in' period that had to be observed, otherwise permanent damage to the engine was a possibility. The same must surely apply to our body machines — the heart, lungs and leg muscles have to be run in. Given time our bodies will often recover from the injuries we inflict upon them!

I was a regular smoker for 30-odd years and finally gave up the habit in 1979. During that period my calculator tells me that my lungs inhaled over a quarter million cigarettes! So smokers, providing you give up the habit you can run marathons! It took me ten months to improve from zero to the London Marathon, and 2½ years from zero to this 2,354-mile adventure. Throughout, I followed a careful schedule that trained my body to accept these greater distances, and the rewards for this rigorous training is enjoyment and very few injury problems.

For those runners looking for something a little different and perhaps less competitive, they can always find or invent their own personal routes and challenges. One option could be one of Britain's network of long distance paths, such as Offa's Dyke Path from Chepstow to Prestatyn (167 miles), Pennine Way Path from Edale to Kirk Yetholm (250 miles) or South Down Way from Petersfield to Eastbourne (80 miles), all three being holiday or very long weekend runs! Few of us are good enough athletes to be interested in records, but we can set our own targets and if we give our very best efforts then the results should give us, and often others, a lot of pleasure and personal satisfaction. A good example is the London Marathon where the sheer joy is so often written on the competitors' faces as they cross that finishing line in 2-30-00 or 4-30-00. It depends on their particular handicaps and level of achievement. Always remember that

Chinese proverb: 'The longest journey starts with a single step'!

In 1985 I competed in the 80-mile South Downs Way race from Petersfield to Eastbourne. I completed the course in 99th position from the 376 competitors who survived the distance! My official finishing time was 16 hours 56 minutes 25 seconds. And in 1988 I was fortunate in being credited with a plaque for '1st man over 60' in the Oxford Half-Marathon. My position was 423rd from 2,124 runners. The event started and finished in the Parks near Keble College, where my father had played cricket for the university as an undergraduate before the First World War.